Underwood & Underwood

HARVEY S. FIRESTONE
The Man Who Rediscovered Liberia

LIBERIA
REDISCOVERED

By
James C. Young

Garden City   *New York*

DOUBLEDAY, DORAN & COMPANY, INC.

1934

PRINTED AT THE *Country Life Press*, GARDEN CITY, N. Y., U. S. A.

COPYRIGHT, 1934
BY DOUBLEDAY, DORAN & COMPANY, INC.
ALL RIGHTS RESERVED

FIRST EDITION

DT
635
.Y6

FOREWORD

I T WAS only yesterday, as time goes, that Americans reached out into the wide avenues of world production. In the main we still are buyers and sellers abroad, rather than manufacturers, and we seldom undertake to produce raw materials in foreign fields.

This book is intended to present a brief history of the little known Negro Republic of Liberia, a nation in miniature, established by freed American slaves at the western extremity of Africa more than a hundred years ago. From its inception Liberia has been regarded as a moral protectorate of the United States and throughout its troubled history has received our support and encouragement. It is the one nation in the world which may be considered an outgrowth of American institutions and its struggles to survive have had an enduring hold upon the sympathetic interest of the American people. By reason of its friendly traditions and American background, Harvey S. Firestone chose this out-of-

v

38449

the-way corner of the earth as the place to develop an independent source of rubber which would assure protection for American industry from foreign monopoly.

As long ago as 1922 it was demonstrated that the production and price of rubber could be regulated by British growers of the Far East, with governmental support. Only the refusal of Dutch planters in Java and nearby islands, who declined to join the British, brought about collapse of the plan six years after it was launched. That plan has become historical as the first great effort of modern times to restrict the natural use of a product springing from the soil. Now the growers of eleven rubber lands, including the Dutch, have banded together in a new and greater effort to bring about stimulation of rubber prices.

Such are a few of the threads running through this story of Liberia and rubber, the touch of magic in the age of movement. By a combination of circumstances the Republic of Liberia, brought to international prominence since the Firestone enterprise entered the country, has become one of the trouble spots upon the world map. Today it is a cause of anxiety to the United States, the League of Nations and the principal powers of Europe. Even its continued independence remains an issue not yet determined, as the following pages will indicate.

J. C. Y.

CONTENTS

vii

viii   CONTENTS

ILLUSTRATIONS

LIBERIA REDISCOVERED

Chapter I
THE HOME-COMING

RIGHT around the western shoulder of Africa lies Liberia, an outpost upon the Atlantic— Liberia, the rich, the undeveloped, the almost undiscovered until a few years ago. But in those years the name has loomed from newspaper pages until it has a familiar look to the American eye. Today Liberia not only suggests the Negro's most important experiment in self-government, but the greatest effort by American business to develop a primitive land.

The very name of Liberia calls up so much of history that the mind gropes a little to remember. Perhaps it will be as well to define a fact or two. The country begins a short way north of the African corner, up at Mano River, and extends down to the Cavalla River, between four degrees, twenty-two minutes, and eight degrees, thirty-three minutes north of the Equator. If we should draw a line a little south and a little west from

Leicester Square in London it would just about touch the center of Monrovia in Liberia. Or if the line should be drawn westward from Monrovia, it would touch Panama.

The atlases give Liberia 350 miles of coast and a hinterland varying from 100 to 150 miles in width, or an area of 42,000 square miles, about the size of Ohio. Not a large country, but one of special concern to the United States for a hundred years. Along the whole of its length there is no harbor worth while. The surf breaks in tumult upon every mile of its coast, guarded by reefs and sand bars. The several rivers bring down deposits of silt that block every passage. From end to end it is a dangerous coast, where native boats go shooting through inlets or over the sand bars as chance permits.

Nature has shielded Liberia well from approach by the sea. When a steamship comes to port she must slip her chain a mile or two off Monrovia, since no ship of any draft can get inside the troublesome bar. And there is no better spot to anchor along the coast—that long, surfbound coast marked by rugged headlands, where palms wave in the soft air, also seeming to guard the mystery that is Africa.

The Negro Republic stands alone, an independent state upon a continent of colonies. Only Abyssinia, near the Red Sea, may lay claim to a like independence. The British hold Sierra Leone, first colony to the north and west of Liberia, the

French Ivory Coast is to the east and the Atlantic Ocean to the south. At the back French Guinea surrounds the lone Republic of the entire African continent. If we are to believe the geographers this western tip of Africa once fitted into the wide gap of eastern South America, when the two continents were one. That was a long time ago, in the Tertiary epoch—if at all—and the wide Atlantic has rolled between uncounted ages.

Since the day that a band of freed slaves from America set foot in the country, more than a century before our time, Liberia has been a ward of the United States. As the Pilgrims once turned faces westward, bound for Plymouth, so these faced the east. Their adventure was as great, the perils as numerous. And such a coast whereon to plant a new home! From its early discovery by the Portuguese in the fifteenth century it was called the Grain Coast, by reason of a special kind of pepper which traders brought from there to Europe. Later it bore the dreadful name of Slave Coast—a hunting ground for the slavers of New England and Europe.

The conception and evolution of Liberia from its origin to the present day is a part of the American epic. One cannot be told without recognition of the other. From about the time of our Revolution, and to some extent before then, a growing number of slaveholders freed their Negroes for faithful service. Others declared them free by the terms of their wills. This was a last earthly gesture and one indulged in by a number of eminent Americans, including no less a man than George Washington.

In this way, by degrees, a numerous class of freedmen was developed. They rather scorned their fellows and were hated in return, their freedom being an example to cause unrest. Neither were they well accepted by the people as a whole. Looked at in any respect their lot was difficult and they attracted the sympathy of Thomas Jefferson, always a man bent toward the liberal side. After several experiments Jefferson and others of his mind decided that the only solution was to establish colonies of freedmen in Africa, the land of their origin.

That was the genesis of the Liberian settlement told in a few lines but the full account would require a substantial volume. Jefferson's plan presented formidable difficulties. In 1817 the American Colonization Society was formed and two years later the Congress of the United States appropriated $100,000 to support the new organization and "for the keep and deportation of the liberated Negroes." Since that time the Society has maintained friendly assistance for Liberia, the ward of America. Incidentally, it is one of the very oldest of American humanitarian societies.

In 1820 the original band of settlers ventured across the Atlantic on board the *Elizabeth*—4,500

remender

miles. They landed at Sherbo Island, near Freetown, Sierra Leone, where the British already had a similar colony. Finding health conditions bad, the colonists wandered down the coast aboard an American naval vessel, finally selecting the site which is now Monrovia. Curiously enough, the strip of territory between Sierra Leone and the French Ivory Coast was about the one bit of West Africa to which some European power had not laid binding claim.

The newcomers settled upon Cape Mesurado, the nearest point to home, as if they would cling there as close as might be to the land they had left. And never was there such a home-coming. The account of their struggle to survive is a chapter of the Negro's story that does him credit. The mere fact of color proving no bond of sympathy, the newcomers found themselves in the midst of perils. How they persevered against the jungle and its denizens, human or otherwise, and finally won a place in the wilds, makes up an impressive story of fortitude.

By degrees the settlers and their leaders came to terms with tribal chiefs roundabout. Their task might have appalled anybody. Jehudi Ashmun, a white American, became the John Smith of the expedition, guiding it through the first years. Between 1822 and 1828 the foundations were laid. By a happy thought, Robert Munroe Harper of Maryland bestowed the name of Liberia upon the country. It has a classical sound, but in fact was his own adaptation of "liberty." Then the Liberians named their capital Monrovia in honor of our fifth President.

Any attempt to understand Liberia must take into account the constant, zealous efforts in its behalf by American religious and philanthropic groups. They have spent many millions of dollars, averaging $250,000 a year in recent times, for Liberian missions and social services. From the day that the colonists landed, throughout a century, these groups have kept protecting arms around the country and its people. No crisis has arisen in which they were not ready to assist and their interest today continues as active as ever.

After the first venture in 1820 other colonists arrived. Some of them went farther down the coast and there planted another reminder of home—giving the name of Maryland to their colony, upon that distant shore. The joint enterprise prospered against every hazard, including attacks by the natives, sickness and privation. Many died; some lived. In 1847 the American Colonization Society ceded the territory previously acquired and Liberia declared itself to be a Republic, setting up a Constitution like our own. Other nations made no open objections and Liberia was recognized by most of them.

But the next decade or two saw a growth of frontier disputes with France and Great Britain, which controlled the adjacent territory then as now. In less than forty years from the foundation

of the little Negro Republic the two powers, by
their action of 1885, limited Liberian frontiers
to the Mano and the Cavalla rivers. Border
lines in the hinterland were less well defined and
seven years later further encroachments took
place, despite representations by the United
States. And as recently as the early years of this
century Liberia lost additional territory to which
she laid claim.

As events developed the Republic was subjected to threatening gestures, accompanied by
protests from the French and British that Liberian tribes periodically raided the territories
of adjoining colonies. Early in 1908 the British
Consul stationed in Monrovia demanded of
Liberia that the Government organize an armed
Frontier Force under European command, to
check this raiding. Up to that time the only
defensive force of the country had been its police
and militia reserve.

The British demand resulted in an act of the
Liberian Legislature, bearing date of February
6, 1908, which established a Frontier Force. One
Major Cadell, formerly a British officer, was
appointed to command. He ordered arms and
ammunition from London and enrolled a number
of natives who had seen service in the British
regiments of Sierra Leone. Within a short time
the Frontier Force grew into an imposing organization.

This trend of events was not pleasing in French

eyes. Their Vice-Consul objected to the Liberian Government that the Frontier Force was a "British army of occupation" and he in turn demanded the enrollment of French officers and French subjects in numbers equal to the British.

There the matter rested for a while, Major Cadell assuming yet greater authority, including direction of the Monrovia police. The Liberian Government could delay action no longer and asked that he resign, which he declined to do. So insecure was the position of the Government that it did not dare to risk expulsion of the Major or his British native troops. From the other side the French pressed for recognition and a French medical officer was appointed to the Frontier Force.

Here was a new cause of friction. Another British officer serving under Major Cadell presented a note to the Monrovian Government, which he represented as emanating from London, this note being a protest against the presence of any French officer in the Frontier Force. At last the Liberian Legislature was compelled to risk the consequences and dismissed Major Cadell, naming a Liberian Colonel in his stead.

As the Major stepped out he warned the Monrovian Government that mutiny was brewing in the Frontier Force by reason of uncollected back pay and other grievances. The British Government received similar warning and the day before a mutiny actually did take place a

Monrovia, the Capital; the Legislative Hall, and Parade of the Frontier Force

Only Carriers with Hammocks Can Penetrate to the Interior Along Narrow Trails

British warship steamed into the harbor, her guns turned threateningly toward shore. Meanwhile a British regiment waited under arms in Sierra Leone with sailing orders for Monrovia. But the Liberian Government called out the militia and put down the mutiny.

This series of developments, accompanied by internal troubles of many kinds, led the Government to request American assistance as a means of ". . . maintaining the independence of the Republic." President Theodore Roosevelt had shown interest in Liberian affairs and the nation's appeal stirred his sympathy. He determined to send out a commission to study conditions at first hand, but the end of his own term left the appointment to President William Howard Taft, who also looked with sympathy upon Liberian problems. The three members of this commission sailed for Monrovia in April of 1909, aboard a United States cruiser, and remained there some time.

Concerning the mutiny and its possible consequences, the commission afterward observed: "But for the prompt and judicious action of the Liberian Executive, aided by the American Minister resident, the following would presently have been the situation: a British gun-boat in the harbor, a British officer in command of the Frontier Force and a large number of British subjects among the enlisted men, a British official in charge of the Liberian customs, a

British officer in command of the Liberian gunboat *Lark,* a British regiment in the streets of
Monrovia. . . ."

President Taft's investigators found the Republic gravely troubled by complications growing out of its foreign loans. As early as 1871
Liberia had become a borrower of European
money. When the commission began its work
most of these obligations were concentrated in
British hands, and by reason of the frontier
and other difficulties, the Liberian attitude of
mind was distinctly unfriendly to Britain.

Customs revenues had been assigned to
guarantee payment of outside loans, their collection being supervised by two European
officials appointed upon recommendation of the
British Government. When Liberian relations
grew worse rather than better, the British
Government demanded that Liberia name three
additional British officials to its Customs administration and reform its Treasury and courts.

The Republic accepted these terms, but apparently they were not very effective. According
to the American commission of 1909, as officially
stated in its report to President Taft, the plan
as laid down failed of realization and in the early
part of 1909 it came to a sudden stop.

The commission delved deeply into Liberian
troubles, concluding that although the country
needed assistance, Britain was disqualified for
such help because of the "spirit of great bitter-

ness" in Liberia against the British. Furthermore
France had protested the acts of British advisers
in Liberian affairs. In its report the commission
said: "If Liberia is to be dismembered, France
wants a share in it. . . . It is generally believed in
Liberia that Germany has been biding her time
till she could undertake with good grace an
intervention in Liberian affairs."

In endeavoring to adjust the tangled problems
of the country, the commission outlined civic,
administrative and financial reforms, adding the
significant suggestion that the United States
should establish a naval coaling station there.
The American Government next tried to arrange
a private loan for Liberia, but failed, owing
principally to the attitude of foreign powers. The
British, Germans and French were as one in
seeking to maintain their participation in
Liberian affairs. Finally, after two years of
long drawn discussion, an international loan of
$1,700,000 was arranged in 1912 under a Customs
Receivership, with an American as General
Receiver, assisted by French, German and British Receivers.

Here was the setting for an international
drama of intense interest and there was to be
rapid shifting of the scenes. Upon the outbreak
of war in 1914, Liberia assumed even greater
value. The German cable station in Monrovia
was a prize of war much to be desired. The
country produces palm oil in quantities and

palm oil is essential to the making of munitions. While Germany tried to hold her own the Allies eagerly grasped for cable and oil.

The Government in Monrovia was about to find itself in the unpleasant position of trying to prevent seizure from without and at the same time strive to preserve integrity within against tribal rebellion. Once more the United States was implored to aid and the U.S.S. *Chester* arrived at Monrovia in November of 1915. The "moral assistance" of the *Chester* was vital to the Liberian Government as the presence of the cruiser helped to pacify internal troubles and not improbably prevented foreign intervention.

As the war advanced, and mostly by reason of American influence, Liberia declared herself a belligerent upon the Allied side. Since the United States, Liberia and the Allies now were all upon the same side, and the United States being the war chest, our Treasury established a credit of $5,000,000 in favor of Liberia under the Second Liberty Loan Act of September 24, 1917. Liberia got the credit, if not the money. In November of the next year the French and British were notified that under an amendment to the 1912 loan agreement, the United States intended to convert the loan and its administration into an "all-American receivership," controlling internal as well as external revenue.

Still Liberia waited for the money. When the war ended and her chances further diminished,

Secretary of State, Charles E. Hughes, made strong recommendations to Congress, declaring that ". . . to default on one's word in such a case would be regarded among business men in private affairs as very sharp practice, and I felt that it was our duty to go ahead, and I so informed the President."

In an effort to obtain the money Liberia sent a commission to the United States, but Congress passed an act prohibiting the extension of further war loans. To this day Liberia is waiting for the $5,000,000 authorized but never advanced. The country was to stand still until private American enterprise undertook to find a way out.

Chapter II
RUBBER IN THE NEW ERA

MANY new things developed with the twentieth century. One of them was the need for rubber, the indispensable commodity in this age of movement. Early in the century the horseless carriage began to replace Dobbin and the famous shay. From the iron tires of other days there was swift evolution to solid rubber tires, then to pneumatic. The world took to riding upon air—and liked it.

The new age of transportation went forward at an astonishing rate. For seventy-five years Americans had thought in terms of railroads, not highways. Post roads of former times were all but abandoned and hardly ever used except for local traffic. Then, suddenly, the paved streets of the cities were extended into the country, from city to city. Horseless carriages traveled such unheard of distances as a hundred miles in a single day. Any man could see that gasoline and rubber were the two great necessities of to-morrow.

That was about the stage of evolution when the World War broke with a fury unknown to civilization. The army which could travel the swiftest had much the best chance of victory. Rubber again—plus gasoline. The protracted struggle was to put rubber upon a gold basis. Without it, the movements of army transport proved impossible. Cut off from rubber, Germany suffered intensely, exhausting her technical skill in the effort to produce synthetic rubber. A truck tire was worth more than a gun.

Then the end of the conflict brought a lull in production of every kind. It was certain that the uses for rubber in the pursuits of peace would exceed those of war. But the world came to a pause in the Summer of 1920 and that pause grew into a fair-sized depression, continuing until the Fall of 1921. Before that time there never was enough rubber to supply the demand. But the 300,000 tons then in warehouses created an unmanageable surplus, driving down the world price.

Three fourths of the rubber growing areas were in the Far East under the British flag and the planters bitterly protested when the price dropped to fourteen cents a pound. Production methods were geared to a higher price level and there had been only slight attempts to retrench.

The planters saw no prospect of any considerable increase in price and in this situation the British growers became conscious that they held three fourths of the producing area in their hands. They got a prompt hearing in London. Winston Churchill, an ambitious man and one ever given to large plans, took up their cause, proclaiming that, "One of our principal means of paying our debt to the United States is in the provision of rubber." As Secretary of State for the Colonies he was able to lend powerful aid.

A Parliamentary committee conducted inquiries, the result of its studies being the Stevenson Rubber Restriction Act, effective November 1, 1922. Under its terms the Governor-in-Council of Malaysia received power to make and enforce rules controlling rubber exports, in this way seeking to create artificially high prices. When the market for rubber was fourteen cents a pound, the Stevenson Act established an official "fair price" of thirty-six cents a pound, later increased to forty-two and forty-eight cents, but the actual price touched $1.23 a pound in July of 1925.

No other piece of marketing legislation has caused quite the disturbance brought about by the Stevenson Act. The United States, at that time using three fourths of all the rubber produced, and with an expanding demand, confronted an intrenched monopoly.

Among all the necessities of the modern world rubber was the one irreplacable commodity for which no commercial substitute had been found.

Without rubber most of the highway transportation of America must stop, and with it so rich a part of our national life, which flows back and forth along the highways, across the breadth of a continent. Yet every motor wheel that turned in the United States was dependent upon rubber grown in the Far East and controlled by foreign powers, as it still is dependent to this day. In an emergency the supply could be seriously curtailed, if not instantly shut off. It is impressive to remember that we have only enough rubber in warehouses to operate our 24,000,000 motor vehicles three to six months. There is a floating argosy of rubber constantly upon the way that must be transported 10,000 miles or farther for American needs. Any one of a half dozen powers could check this movement, and soon stop the wheels of our motor transport.

When we look back to the first days of the restriction act it is surprising that there was no immediate organized opposition by the industry at large. Only one man stepped forward to challenge the right of any nation to put such a burden upon another. That man was Harvey S. Firestone, known to the American people not alone by reason of his great industrial organization, but emphatically by reason of his stand for fair play in every case.

The Stevenson Act hardly was in operation when Mr. Firestone condemned this measure, which restricted the normal use of a commodity so universally necessary. Then he undertook to organize the American rubber industry in protest. The industry not only failed to respond but there was some opposition from that source. He carried the fight to Washington, established offices there, and prompted the introduction of a bill in Congress appropriating $500,000 for the investigation and development of new sources of rubber free of European monopoly. Within thirty days this bill was passed by the House and Senate without a dissenting vote.

Soon afterward the Department of Agriculture began experiments with rubber plants that might be grown in the United States. The Department of Commerce organized and sent overseas expeditions to examine promising sources of rubber. Mr. Firestone, realizing that the situation was grave and likely to become critical, determined to begin an independent search for neutral rubber lands.

Actually there was only one man in the fight against foreign domination and he appeared to have a poor chance, yet he kept after the restriction act day by day. "The law is basically and economically unsound," he said. "Americans should produce their own rubber."

Each time that the commodity was advanced a penny a pound it cost the American people $8,000,000. In the six years that the act remained in force their total bill amounted to

$1,250,000,000 more than they would have paid had the market continued at fourteen cents, the price when the act became effective.

Along with the development of rubber goes a story of modern treasure. The first supplies originated in the wilds of Brazil, which gave its name to the preferred variety, *Hevea Brasiliensis*. From an early time the fact was suspected in South America that rubber had unusual and highly valuable qualities. One of the first practical uses was the waterproof coat known as a Mackintosh down to our time. Brazil, foreseeing wealth, forbade any one to take Hevea seeds out of the country, under a rigid embargo.

But in 1876 an English botanist and traveler then in Brazil, Henry A. Wickham, risked the penalty to bring away some of the seeds. They were carefully tended in Kew Gardens, near London, the most famous of botanic gardens, where the precious seeds sprang into tiny rubber trees. These were transplanted to the Far East, there to develop into the rubber empire of later times, bringing to Britain the wealth that Brazil once visioned.

It was not long until the wild rubber from South America and Africa lost its importance, the cultivated product of British and Dutch East Indian plantations becoming the sole dependable supply. In the easy American way we went blithely along, confident that there would be

plenty of rubber at a reasonable price. Suddenly
the corner was on and the nation paid the piper,
though it hardly enjoyed the dance.

Harvey S. Firestone saw more clearly every
day that he could not depend upon the American
Government alone to find new sources. No matter how earnest the Government's efforts, the
undertaking was bound to be protracted. Government assistance might be valuable in time but
the need became more urgent every hour.

Attention turned to Central and South America. Mexico was a friendly neighbor right at
hand. As long ago as 1910, during the first rubber
boom, a number of Brazilian rubber trees had
been planted in the Mexican state of Chiapas to
see what the results might be. And Chiapas was
no more than 500 miles from the Texas border,
practically at home.

Mr. Firestone dispatched an expedition to
inspect the country and not long afterward
leased a plantation of 35,000 acres, bearing the
Castilloa Elastica rubber tree as well as the *Hevea
Brasiliensis*. Although these trees grew to natural
size, they failed to give a normal yield of the
milky latex containing rubber. They were or-
phaned trees in a far land. Labor and governmental conditions also proving unfavorable, the
enterprise was abandoned, but this undertaking
again confirmed that the preferred Hevea trees
would not yield rubber commercially more than
600 miles from the Equator.

Next the Philippines held attention. Harvey S. Firestone, Jr., and a group of rubber men and engineers sailed for Manila in January of 1926. The Philippines were just across the Pacific, so to speak, and there the American flag assured a fair competitive chance.

Intensive search soon was under way. The Firestone party proceeded to visit the islands, among them Mindanao, famous stronghold of the Moros. They found both a welcome and abundance of land adapted to rubber. Then a real obstacle developed, in the form of a Philippine law prohibiting any one from owning or controlling more than 2,500 acres of agricultural land.

But the best opinion in the islands assured Mr. Firestone, Jr., that the obstacle could be overcome. Accordingly he prepared a bill known as the Rubber Land Act which was presented to the Philippine Legislature, making it possible to introduce rubber cultivation in the islands upon an adequate basis. Politicians promptly raised the cry that, "Every dollar of American capital is one more nail in the coffin of independence." The Rubber Land Act went the way of many good bills; it died in committee. Such is the reason why the Philippines sacrificed their opportunity to acquire a world industry.

From the Philippines Mr. Firestone, Jr., and his staff continued their survey of rubber lands, going on to Malaya, Sumatra, Java and Sarawak, "the land of the white Rajah," in Borneo. But the place that would meet all needs was yet to be found. One thought persisted. Whatever source of rubber for the United States that Firestone developed must be free from foreign domination and control if such a result could be brought about by human effort.

Chapter III
EDISON EXPLORES THE UNKNOWN

WHILE the search went on in foreign lands, Harvey S. Firestone discussed the subject of rubber supply with his friend Thomas A. Edison, pointing out the dire position in which America would be placed should the course of events curtail or cut off our one source of this vital material. Mr. Edison expressed the belief that rubber could be produced in America; if not rubber trees from the tropics, then rubber-bearing plants found at home or abroad.

Further conferences were held between Mr. Edison, Mr. Ford and Mr. Firestone, with the result that the Edison Botanic Research Corporation was organized. Then the inventor laid aside other experimental work and plunged into the study of rubber with the zeal which had wrested so many tributes from Nature; foreseeing that America would suffer severely if deprived of rubber in a crisis, and inspired by the hope of supplying this need with his own hand.

The story of Mr. Edison's search for rubber that could be cultivated here at home is one of commanding interest. He organized a laboratory and experimental gardens in New Jersey and Florida, but his principal efforts were to be concentrated at his southern home in Fort Myers, Florida.

An impressive vision of the man rises before the eye of the mind as he embarked upon his exploration of the unknown. Chemistry was Mr. Edison's first enthusiasm and throughout his career he had turned to his retorts for diversion. Here was an opportunity for research in a cause that might be critical to the American people.

It was 1925 when he definitely began the study of rubber at close range. By this time the inventor was in his seventy-ninth year and had conferred manifold benefits upon humanity. In turn mankind had extended to him signal honors. Surely there was little that such a man could want and assuredly nothing for himself. But in this late hour of his life he again caught the spark, moved by the will to win a last gift from Nature.

It was a land without frontiers, but many barriers, which he sought to invade. The principle he decided upon was to find a shrub, vine or similar plant yielding rubber latex in sufficient quantity to make regular harvesting practicable. In a general way, science was aware that rubber latex could be found in certain specimens of

Copyright 1931, Gravelle

Thomas A. Edison at Work in His Fort Myers Laboratory; Henry Ford (left) and Harvey S. Firestone (right)

plants; but there never had been any analysis of the subject; no data existed. Mr. Edison began at the beginning, without aid or guide.

One of his first steps was to enlist a number of students and teachers of botany as field commanders. Equipped with trucks and provided with crews of men, they went into all sections of the United States, collecting specimens of plant life. These in turn were transshipped to New Jersey or Florida and by degrees he came into possession of hundreds, then thousands of specimens. Not content with his examination of North American plants, he obtained seeds from Liberia, the Far East and South America and attempted to cultivate each of these varieties in Florida. Some of the foreign plants grew into maturity, more or less, but none of them supplied the precious latex in worth-while quantities.

Steadily the search went on, Mr. Edison becoming so engrossed that he withdrew from all other activities—even a camping trip with his two old friends, Ford and Firestone—and henceforth devoted himself to his search for rubber with the singular application that marked his character. In those busy days his friends observed that the years had fallen away from him. He was back in the full vigor of the '80's and '90's, when he astonished the world—or so it seemed to those who watched him come to grips with Nature.

There were small successes, and just as numerous disappointments. But he found that a con-

siderable number of American plants would yield
rubber latex in a slight degree. The question
became one of pressing importance to find the
plant with the maximum yield. To make this
possible he had to develop a number of laboratory devices and especially a machine which
would grind up the plant specimens before they
could be subjected to chemical processes. Each
step required time and application, but the
inventor toiled happily in his Fort Myers laboratory, finding a path little by little into his land
of the unknown.

He conceived of an ideal plant that would grow
to a good size in six or eight months, and in such
profusion as to be mowed like wheat. Thus his
research had the double purpose of protecting
the American people in a crucial quarter and of
providing a new industry having unlimited
possibilities. No doubt the inventor looked across
those broad fields of rubber plants which he was
going to grow and saw thousands of workers
busy there at the harvest.

After a year or two, the laboratories in New
Jersey and Florida had analyzed and classified
thousands of prospective rubber plants. From
all of these he selected hundreds for cultivation
upon his southern estate and these were reduced
to a few likely varieties. One, in particular,
caught his attention; no less a plant than our
familiar golden rod. Once he had plucked a strip
of bamboo from a palmetto fan and found the

filament that gave us the electric light. Why not a rubber tire from a stalk of golden rod? He began its cultivation with intensive efforts, naming a choice specimen the *Golden Rod Gigantica*. It justified the name, under his care, growing to a greater size, with more abundant leaves than golden rod ever had grown before.

Mr. Edison's delight may be imagined when he found that his new golden rod yielded more latex to the acre than any plant so far analyzed; a yield of seven per cent. This was not the highest yield from the thousands of plants, but it was the largest quantity per acre by reason of the heavy foliage and abundant growth.

There is a distinct touch of pathos in the Edison search for rubber. In all probability he would have adapted a rubber plant to American soil had he been fated to complete his labors. The result literally lay within his grasp, yet a little way removed. At the end of six years he had developed the *Golden Rod Gigantica* and his own laboratory processes to the point of practical vulcanization, as the curing process is termed. Eagerly he exhibited strips of this vulcanized rubber to his friends Ford and Firestone, but the end was at hand.

However, the fruits of his research are not to be wasted. The Department of Agriculture of the United States Government has taken over the records which he left as an endowment for other hands and his work is being carried forward.

Chapter IV
LIBERIA IS REDISCOVERED

T HE world literally lay upon the council table in Akron, where engineers and executives bent over detail maps, studying the country that might be the goal of their quest. All the while other hands had been at work abroad in the search for rubber lands. As early as 1924 a beginning was made in Africa when Donald A. Ross examined Liberian possibilities at the head of a Firestone expedition. Following his favorable preliminary report, Mr. Firestone sent a man from his own office, William D. Hines, to join in the rediscovery of Liberia; whose mission was to investigate the political and economic outlook. Between his arrival in 1924 and the present, a span of ten years, runs this romance of pioneering for rubber. It is an epic unapproached by modern business. For an example upon an equal scale we must turn to the Panama Canal—and that was a Government job—or to the winning of the

west by the railroad builders. Certainly it is
true that American business never before engaged in such an undertaking, waged across far
seas against every obstacle a primitive land could
offer.

A full century had passed since the landing of
the freedmen. A third and fourth generation
stood in the place of the first. These were native
Africans, but the American influence of their
forebears still prevailed and the tradition of
friendship endured as strong as ever. Instinc-
tively every Liberian looks to the United States
as the homeland that will not fail him in time of
need, and the need frequently has proved acute.
Equally the United States has accepted this
responsibility by reason of the exceptional circumstances under which Liberia was founded.
In effect it may be said that the country has been
recognized as a moral protectorate of the United
States. Here, if anywhere upon earth, Americans
could expect opportunity to develop a great
new enterprise without hindrance; in fact, with
all possible aid and encouragement. If this was
not actually American soil under the American
flag, no other soil or flag might be expected to
reflect more of the American spirit.

Added to these considerations were the pledged
assurances of Liberian Government officials that
nothing should be left undone to further the
undertaking. The people themselves showed the
liveliest interest. When they saw that Firestone

was inclined to establish a world enterprise upon
their soil, enthusiasm mounted high. At last—
after a hundred years of struggle—Liberia would
share in a big economic development of the modern day.

A decision to enter Liberia was not one to be
lightly taken. Plainly, this was no ordinary
enterprise, even of overseas business. It assumed
the rank of an adventure. Liberia was a land
undeveloped, practically untouched, but the
natural advantages were exceptional. Proof
abounded that rubber would grow well in this
soil. A British company had planted the 2,000-
acre Mount Barclay Plantation in 1910. Later it
was abandoned and returned to the jungle but
the full grown trees awaited tapping, which the
rubber pioneers were prompt to do. They found
the latex abundant, the yield being unusually
large. Then Liberia was shown to have four dry,
rainless months, followed in some years by as
much as 150 inches of rainfall, two conditions
almost identical with those in the Acre region of
Brazil, native home of the Hevea rubber trees.

Another compelling reason was the ready
supply of labor, easily drawn from a population
of not less than 1,500,000 people. The natives
were found to rank among the best of African
tribes. Their generally cheerful character was
one more recommendation. Although without
exerience they could be expected to learn the
simple duties required. There was an example of

adaptability in the Kru men, known as skilled sailors throughout African waters.

At last Harvey S. Firestone saw his plans about to reach fulfillment. Here, indeed, was the land of his hopes. One day he went down in Wall Street to call upon the bankers and announced that he wanted $100,000,000 to develop an independent source of rubber for the American people. "The British have invested $700,-000,000 in rubber plantations of the Far East and we should not hesitate to invest $100,000,000, as we use more than seventy per cent of the world production," he said. When the bankers politely declined, he resolved to go ahead upon his own account.

This was about the stage of progress when Harvey S. Firestone, Jr., reached Monrovia in September of 1926. Taking up the negotiations, he completed the final phases. A "planting agreement" subsequently was prepared in mutually acceptable form and enacted into law by the Liberian Legislature the 10th day of November, 1926.

This document provides enlightening reading, commanding attention by reason of the co-operative benefits which it confers. The Firestone Plantations Company received the privilege to lease for ninety-nine years up to 1,000,000 acres of land belonging to the public domain of Liberia. In exchange the company bound itself to pay rent of six cents an acre annually for each acre taken over, plus one per cent. export duty upon every pound of rubber shipped, calculated at New York prices.

The rent was based upon the prevailing value of land in the country. The Revised Statutes of Liberia specify that the ". . . Price of land lying on the margin of rivers shall be $1 per acre. Those lying in the interior of the lands on the rivers shall be fifty cents per acre." Six cents an acre annually represented six per cent. upon a $1 valuation from land which had yielded nothing.

At the time of the agreement rubber was worth forty to fifty cents a pound in New York and an average yield of 500 pounds to the acre implied an additional revenue in excess of $2 an acre per annum, derived from the one per cent. export duty. This revenue was at a rate higher than usually required of pioneer enterprises in other rubber lands. By contrast, the Government of Johore, in British Malaya, wishing to encourage the development of rubber plantations, made a grant to Sir Frank Swettenham under the terms of which he obtained lands in perpetuity for an all inclusive charge equivalent to seventeen American cents an acre, paid annually. He was exempted from all duties, and all taxes, present or future. This rate of seventeen cents may be compared with the price of more than $2 a year, which Firestone would pay when the acreage came into production, as based upon rubber prices at the time of the contract.

The planting agreement having been consummated with Liberia, Mr. Firestone, Jr., in an official letter addressed to President C. D. B. King under date of December 2, 1926, required that native labor must have the right to bargain for its own terms and rates of employment, without dictation to such labor by the Government or any other authority. The letter was important as bearing upon later developments and read in part as follows:

"Upon the representations that have been made to the company by the Government during the past year relative to labor, the company offers the following as a supplementary interpretation . . .

"The company may employ any labor or laborers which the company may recruit or which may present themselves to the company at any of its operations or offices for employment, without such labor being first required to obtain permission of, or be registered by, the Government.

"Such labor so employed shall be free to bargain for its terms and conditions of employment with the company and shall be free to sever its employment with the company at its own will and convenience.

"We desire to point out to the Government again that the success of our development in Liberia is largely dependent upon the organization of a permanent and contented labor force.

This can only be done through free and unrestricted employment and upon terms and conditions which are agreeable to the laborers themselves.

"We also desire to inform the Government that its representations regarding labor presented at past conferences have received our utmost consideration and the interpretations suggested herein are put forward in a spirit of coöperation and in accord with the Government's problems."

While the Liberian undertaking decidedly was an uncut page in the Firestone book of experience, the principle was insisted upon that American methods of employment must be observed. Since time immemorial Africa has known forced labor if not outright slavery, more or less disguised in later years. From the beginning Firestone endeavored to set up precautions against the possibility of forced labor without the company's knowledge and certainly without its consent.

Next it became necessary to consider the existing financial condition and economic outlook of Liberia. Neither was encouraging, though not beyond amelioration. Obviously it would have been inviting danger to begin operations in a country so embarrassed by European obligations. There was urgent need for Liberia to set her affairs in order.* As a means of making this possible, Firestone engaged to arrange a refund-

*See Appendix, page 168.

ing loan to pay Liberia's internal and external debts and at the same time to supply capital for pressing needs.

Conferences with the Government eventuated in approval by the Legislature of a loan agreement embracing the terms of assistance. These stipulated that the Finance Corporation of America, organized for the purpose, should lend the needed money through a bond issue, with the National City Bank of New York as fiscal agent. Certain revenues were pledged as security. Liberia was to issue up to $5,000,000 of "External Forty Year Sinking Fund Seven Per Cent. Gold Bonds," of which the Finance Corporation initially would take $2,500,000. The remainder could be offered when ". . . the total annual amount (of revenues) exceeded the sum of $800,000 for two consecutive years."

The reasonable terms of this financing were evidenced by the fact that France and Belgium obtained loans at about the same time and at the same rate. Polish and Bolivian bonds were selling in the market at prices to yield eight per cent.

Monrovia lacked a harbor and, as part of the general development, Firestone undertook to do the dredging and construction necessary for a satisfactory port. By agreement, this work should be completed at a cost not to exceed $300,000, which the Government would repay. Accordingly the J. G. White Engineering Corporation of New York was engaged and more than $115,000 expended in the effort. After prolonged attempts the engineers decided that the shifting sands made the project impracticable except at prohibitive expense. Upon their advice the work was abandoned and the loss absorbed by Firestone, without cost to Liberia. Later on company engineers designed a special type of turtle-back, twin-motored steel lighters for the arduous work of crossing the sandbar, and they do it handsomely in any weather. In fact, they forever render unnecessary huge expenditures otherwise required for construction and maintenance of breakwaters and wharves.

To assist in establishing a business administration for Liberia it was agreed that the President of the United States should nominate, and the President of Liberia appoint, a Financial Adviser to help correct difficulties. The Government granted the Financial Adviser authority to supervise the collection of its revenues and the disbursement of its funds. Furthermore, no floating debt was to be created without his approval.

Should differences develop in interpreting the contracts, after preliminary arbitration that might prove unacceptable to either party, each had the right to demand further arbitration upon terms to be decided by the United States Department of State, such arbitration to be final and complete.

Under these mutually favoring auspices Firestone entered Liberia.

Chapter V

INVADING THE JUNGLE

Akron became the general headquarters, Liberia the front line. Firestone's effort to conquer the Liberian jungle was to prove empire building of the biggest kind and every engineer, each shovel and monkey wrench had to be transported across the Atlantic.

When the rubber men landed no supplies were available in Monrovia, the commerce of the city being in European hands and generally confined to small miscellaneous articles. There was only one road in the country, twenty-six miles long, running from Monrovia to Careysburg and impassable most of the time. For the one road there was one automobile and that belonged to President King. Elsewhere only native trails led into the jungle, a green wall of unbroken expanse.

Monrovia stands upon a bluff, its five principal avenues crossed by eight or ten streets. Here and there a two-story house rises above the general

level of one floor and the better homes are of
concrete or brick, though corrugated iron and
wood are more common. In the dry season bril-
liant sunlight sears this rambling city; in the wet
season there are sheets of rain.

Such was the untouched land that the pioneers
prepared to explore. Anybody could have seen
that they should begin with a river upon their
flank, and the river selected was the Du, which
pours into the Atlantic at the south of Monrovia.
It was a narrow waterway throughout, in some
places no more than a hundred feet wide. Not
only narrow, but dammed with the trunks of
rotting trees fallen there any time in the last
hundred years. Along the banks grew an odd
sort of tree known as the screw pine, its roots extending out into the river, entangling everything.

Carefully the explorers made their way up-
stream, absorbed in the new world opening
before them. After days of observation and investigation they paused at a point now forty
miles from Monrovia by modern highway, but
then lost in the jungle which formed a double
wall along both banks, a green maze without a
single road and hardly a trail worth the name.
Occasionally, in the depths, a village might be
found. But of aid from man or nature, none whatever.

It took courage and imagination to confront
the jungle, armed with no better tools than a
man might carry in his kit.

From the western bank the rubber pioneers pushed into the unknown, finding around them towering trees that rose to a hundred feet and higher. Ross led the advance. Here, almost upon the Equator, everything grew in profusion— entirely too profuse when it was a question of cutting your way through the all but impenetrable mass. Underfoot, rotting vegetation and tangled plant life tripped the invaders at every step. Overhead, giant creepers ran up the trees, lacing them into one fastness.

It must have given the explorers a solemn feeling to go crashing through the still, dark jungle. Truly a place of fascination, of ominous dangers. Also a place of charm, of wonder. Around them they found specimens of trees that no one of them had seen before. In open spots vividly colored flowers grew in rank abundance and frequently of varieties that nobody could name. Then there were swarms of birds, tinted as only tropical birds can be tinted, and many of these were as little known as the trees or flowers. Every leaf that rustled might conceal a strange creature, or one ferocious; maybe a deadly serpent like the green mamba, or a chance boa constrictor.

The exploring party included soil experts and numerous specialists. Each man went to work in his own way, seeking to reveal the jungle's secrets; especially to learn if this was the promised land for a future empire of rubber.

It was not long until Ross called a campfire

council, where every man reported. With the eye of fancy we can see, at this distance, that intent circle lighted by the flickering fire. It is not hard to hear the question and answer, the pro and con of their discussion. One after another they counted the advantages, the disadvantages. In this way, with the smoke of their pipes curling up into the tropic night, a decision was made. Here was the place to begin.

A little way off several villages were found where labor might be obtained. With the help of tribal chiefs the original working force was brought together and the adventure began to take on organized form. Native crews were selected, under proper leadership, to blaze trails a quarter of a mile apart, starting from the river bank. Following a compass line and clearing a way as they went, these crews cut paths into the green depths. Cross paths came next, dividing the jungle into forty-acre sections.

Added to the engineers' full measure of trouble were the obstructions under water in the Du. Before they could grapple with the real task they had to enlist native swimmers who would dive below by the hour, to hack at water-logged trunks with keen machetes. Three long months of this and the Du became passable for canoes.

While development along the Du went forward a second group of explorers launched operations upon the bank of the Cavalla River, at the southern tip of Liberia, near Cape Palmas.

Operations of '27–'28 expanded in many directions and the methods then employed may be taken as typical of the successive stages of development from virgin jungle to planted rubber.

Meanwhile, G. H. Q., in Akron was as busy as any army base ever could have been, training and sending men overseas, but an army of a different sort and for a different purpose. Selections were made of graduates representing a dozen colleges, men experienced in engineering, forestry, plant pathology and essential sciences. The higher command went to technicians of established rank. As they arrived in Liberia, followed by their staffs, the country witnessed a burst of activity such as it never had seen before in its drowsy century of life.

Everything required, down to the most ordinary tools, had to be transported from Europe or America. When shipments from Akron arrived via London the distance was 7,000 miles instead of the 5,000 from Akron direct. In the beginning even water—bottled mineral water—was shipped across the Atlantic. Later the pioneers sunk the first wells ever drilled in the country.

For a while they lived in shacks or slept upon the ground underneath the stars. As development advanced the question arose of building permanent homes. Apparently a simple undertaking. Nothing to do but level the timber. But, there was not a sawmill in the country until Firestone came, and scarcely a saw. One of the

earliest shipments was a lot of two-man saws,
made by a noted concern back home. Those
saws were tough and sharp, yet most of them
were returned to America before long for repairs.
The ironwood of the jungle defied even steel
saws and chilled steel axes sometimes chipped
in the hands that wielded them.

After a while a full-fledged sawmill arrived and
with it came caterpillar tractors to haul the
trunks to the mill. Soon the rip of an American
saw tearing through timber broke the jungle
quiet. Bungalows began to appear, some of wood,
some of concrete blocks molded upon the spot.
The natives showed themselves adept in this
work, having become more than fair masons by
reason of the training gained in building their
huts of dried clay.

During the rainy season thousands of men
thronged to the plantations, offering to take a
hand in felling the heavy jungle growth, which
had to be cleared before planting could begin.
Sometimes they traveled for days, led by a sub-
chief, who stayed on to look after their welfare.
This trip along the dim trails was a novel experience to the majority, as the Liberian native
usually keeps close to his village. Most of them
never had been so far from home before. They
arrived with the enthusiasm of children, de-
lighted to see the new sights and to enter upon
the new kind of life.

Groups of about 200 men were assigned to

common plots of ground and given time and materials to build their own houses in their own way. From the first it was realized that interference with the fundamentals of native life should be avoided, but there has been a consistent effort to improve the sanitation of these native villages and gradually to impart instruction in a better way of living.

Uniformly the natives showed themselves to be good-natured fellows, always curious about the ways of the white man, but ready to do their utmost. The wages of a shilling a day—twenty-four cents—were the first that most of them had received and equal to those paid in the rubber fields of the Far East. Besides, the Firestone payroll was the first real payroll ever known to the country and a regular pay day within the fringe of the jungle opened broad vistas before Liberian eyes. Up to that time the West African colonies of certain European nations had utilized the country's surplus of labor for their own development, and not always with advantage to the natives. It is a somewhat curious fact that this circumscribed little country should be more densely populated than adjacent colonies but with less opportunity for employment than any of them.

Throughout the rainy season of 1927, from May until October, the axe and the saw were hard at work, plied by willing hands. One after another age-old trunks fell to earth. By the end of the rainy period a wide area had been cleared and when the next dry season reached its height, in January of '28, the torch was applied.

It stirs the fancy to think of that blaze sweeping over miles upon miles of fallen timber, sending up a storm cloud of smoke riven by fire. Wild life fled to the uttermost parts. The smoke mounted in vast, billowing clouds and spread across the horizon until it obscured the sun, exactly as though it had been in eclipse. Every January a dry, burning wind sweeps over Liberia from the distant Sahara, bringing with it a desert rain of fine sand. This wind is known as the harmattan and is much dreaded. When the population of Monrovia saw the clouds of smoke that hovered over the burning jungle miles away they thought the harmattan surely was upon them.

Only desolation remained in the pathway of the fire, but a desolation that presaged a new day. In places the tough old trunks survived the flames and had to be burned again. Once they were destroyed, yet another task awaited and truly a task of no mean order, the removal of the charred débris. When this at last was accomplished the rubber men found their long-sought plantations ready for planting, which was to prove a delicate process. First a series of holes two feet square and four feet deep had to be sunk fifteen feet apart, then filled with top soil. After a few days of rain and the settling of the soil, a

A Firefront Miles Long to Blaze the Way for Rubber Planting

Women Rice Beaters Preparing for Tomorrow's Dinner

young rubber tree from the nursery could be
planted in each hole. From that time the planted
area was zealously weeded to prevent choking
of the seedlings, and also guarded against small
animals which would devour the bark and leaves.

Until 1928 selected rubber seedlings were
planted, which would grow into mature trees
within five or six years, annually yielding up to
500 pounds an acre. However, by that time,
progress in budgrafting methods had developed
in the Far East to a point which promised a yield
of as much as 2,000 pounds an acre annually.

Accordingly the Firestone plant pathologist
was dispatched to Far Eastern rubber centers,
with instructions to return posthaste, bringing
the finest "clones" available. This unfamiliar
word calls up an aspect of biological life that it
may be as well to explain. After the World War
plantation owners, striving to obtain a larger
yield per acre, endeavored to increase quantity
by scientific methods. Experience showed that
certain trees would provide a larger annual yield
than others. Then it was learned that the offshoots of some trees could transmit the high
yielding characteristics of their mother tree. The
whole bud family of a mother tree is described as
a "clone." The clones in which the offshoots are
capable of transmitting the yield characteristics
of the mother tree become known as "proven
clones."

In September of '28 the Firestone pathologist

returned to Liberia, bringing a selection of "budded" stock from the best proven clones of the Far East. These were planted in prepared beds and twelve long months afterward their new buds were ready for grafting to seedlings in multiplication nurseries. A further wait of eight to ten months and the slender stems of the budded seedlings could be cut, when they likewise became "budwood," each piece bearing twenty to thirty buds.

The ensuing process of grafting required much practice and skill and the native entrusted with the work had to be specially trained. As a first step he would cut an incision in the bark of a tree about to be "budded"; a three-sided incision close to the ground. Next the native would trim a piece of bark with a bud attached from the budwood in his hand. Then the flap of bark over the incision could be pulled up just enough to insert the fresh bud underneath the bark. Afterward it was securely bound in place.

This did not represent the end of the operation, by any means. A splint of bamboo next was placed over the incision, in about the way that a surgeon would bind a wound, and this splint fastened with a single loop of wire. Finally it was necessary to close the edges of the incision with a waterproofing substance such as beeswax or tar in order to keep out moisture and insects.

Three weeks later the wire and bamboo splint could be removed and the bark gently raised to determine whether germination had taken place. If not successful, the process must be repeated until germination did come about. Then the original trunk of the tree was severed a little way above the graft and a coating of waterproof substance applied to the stump.

And that, briefly, is the way millions of rubber trees are being budgrafted in far away Liberia.

Chapter VI

RADIO LINKS AMERICA TO LIBERIA

Now the radio was to bring its humanizing touch to the hinterland of Liberia. No mere description could make plain the efforts put forth by the Akron base or at the front deep in the jungle as Firestone's pioneering activities developed in breadth and variety. Yet the interior of Liberia was about as difficult of access as any place could have been. With luck, mail might reach the United States from Monrovia in three weeks, though a month was nearer the average, and cablegrams via Europe were extremely costly for such a purpose. The interior itself was yet farther away. Only the radio could meet the need and the attempt to join northern Ohio to western Africa was to be another pioneering job of impressive difficulties.

Radio communication across the Atlantic and the Pacific had been established through high-powered stations operating upon long wave lengths. The Firestone problem must be met with short wave lengths or not at all, and the harnessing of the short wave had been such a recent advance that the method was not well understood.

Here again a new undertaking offered a challenge. The organization in Liberia had been all but isolated from headquarters. Every thought and impulse between the base and the men in the field must pass through roundabout channels. Radio was the imperative need, yet radio itself was such a new thing, in the practical sense, that half of its vagaries were a mystery from which no hand had drawn the screen. Short wave communication represented an uncharted void.

The Akron laboratories concentrated their resources upon the new requirement. Lying only a few degrees above the Equator, Liberia was subject to atmospheric disturbances which seriously interfered with attempts to open communication between the continents. Experiments covered a large number of wave lengths, seeking the particular wave best adapted to this tropical climate. To establish contact between the Equator and a northern city, then to "keep the line open" across the width of the Atlantic, was an undertaking of the first order.

Gradually these problems began to yield under scientific examination. After months of effort the necessary apparatus was completed. Experimentally it was bound to work; the real test lay ahead. When the station reached Africa, in an assortment of packing cases, it was sent up the Du to the plantation, where there had been only lush jungle a year or so before. By this time it was an immense clearing partly planted with rubber seedlings. And there a modern radio station soon raised its towers toward the sky.

One of the early obstacles proved to be a "dead spot" somewhere in the ether that defied transmission. As often as Liberia tried to call Akron, just as often the dead spot intervened and signals faded out. It was well known that radio waves travel in an arc and each one selected rose to a different pitch, the object being to find a wave which would rise above the "dead spot." As this troublesome area might be hundreds of miles in width and breadth and of an unknown height, it required nice discrimination to find a wave operating to the best advantage at a particular moment. But in time the selected wave lengths were brought under control and everything made ready for the installation of service.

It was a great day, March 18, 1928, when Harvey S. Firestone, Jr., then in Liberia, sent the first message to his father in Akron; a day to bear a red mark, bringing the two countries into direct communication. The days and months of delay, uncertainty, were wiped out with one gesture connecting America to Liberia, a quarter

way around the globe. From that time the head
of the house, back in Akron, literally might say
to his secretary, "Just ask how things are going
down on the plantations today," and have the
answer back within an hour.

As 1928 drew to a close the station upon the
Du reached effective working order, a direct tie
between Akron and the jungle, where a new world
was in the making. By the touch of a key this
far frontier came into instant contact with the
center of industrial America. After ages of
isolation, of which the last day was much like
the first, radio linked this jungle land to the
modern day.

What radio was to mean to Firestone in Liberia
has proved past the telling. Since service began,
headquarters in Akron and outposts in Africa
have maintained daily contact. This service was
to prove an immeasurable gain both to the
Firestone enterprise and the west coast of Africa.
No other practicable radio had existed between
West Africa and the United States or Europe.
Once communication was shown to be feasible,
the United States-Liberia Radio Corporation
was organized, offering regular commercial service to the public.

In the holiday time of that year Mr. Firestone
determined to bring his whole organization together for a half hour of one evening. Plans were
laid for a world wide broadcast of his personal
New Year's greeting. This was to be one of the

very first, if not actually the first, short wave
broadcast attempted upon such a scale.

The Firestone organization in many lands received notice that an international family gathering would be held by means of radio. Certainly
this news was received with interest everywhere
but nowhere with livelier anticipation than in
Liberia.

So many new and unusual things had been
introduced since the arrival of Firestone that the
natives had become more or less prepared for
innovations which seemed strange indeed to
them. But when they were told that the white
men promised to bring the sound of music and
voices across the sea they thought that this time
they were about to be deceived. Even had they
believed that sound could travel so far, the width
of the Atlantic was beyond their conception. To
them, the land from which the white men came
was somewhere off the African shore, but not
far away.

For days the plantation forces talked of nothing else, though most of them doubted that this
magic would work. Sagely they shook knowing
heads, since it was plain that nobody could do
such a thing except by the aid of sorcery greater
than their best witch doctors could command.
Yet they decided among themselves to wait and
see. So often they had found the white men able
to do astonishing things that this supreme bit of
magic might be at least a possibility.

The weekly Firestone program was to go on the air at 8:30 and continue until 9 P.M. which meant 1:30 to 2 A.M. the following morning in Liberia. Ordinarily communication between Akron and the Du was carried on in Morse code, but special apparatus, installed for this event, rested upon a table outside the station in Liberia.

When the expected moment arrived every member of the staff who could get there had gathered around the station, in the center of the Du development. Back of them were thousands of natives, curiously waiting to see what might happen. It was one of those moon-flooded nights such as Africa alone may know; a canopy of stars stretching across the heavens. From the jungle came the boom of croaking frogs and a medley of night noises. The natives had brought drums and harps as there must be music at every gathering of theirs. Until they saw what the white men might be about they came prepared to supply their own diversion. So the throbbing of drums and the thrumming of harps were joined to the chorus of the tropic night.

This throng was a skeptical audience. Foreseeing still another source of competition, the witch doctors warned the plantation workers that the supposed voices from overseas in reality would not come out of the air, but the sounds, if any were heard, would be just another example of the white men's false "ju ju." Ventriloquism is a leading art of the witch doctors as some of them can throw their voices about in the weirdest manner imaginable. And it was no part of their plans to let the white men rob them of prestige.

While waiting for the promised magic the assembled natives chattered along in lively fashion until there was a crackle of static, when silent wonder settled upon them. Then, clearly, came the sound of music, followed by the voice of Mr. Firestone, conveying his New Year's message from his winter home at Miami Beach in Florida. Even the members of the staff caught the spell. What experience could be stranger than to hear his words borne across thousands of miles as they stood there in distant Africa, but transported for a moment to the land of home. Many of them were known to him personally and they said afterward that the familiar tones of his voice sounded as though he spoke close by. But the natives were differently affected. At his first words some of the women and the more timid souls among the men ran away, and a few never could be induced to come back. Others crawled under the table to see who might be hiding there, talking through the horns. The very bravest strode right up to the broadcasting apparatus to defy this new kind of witch.

The half hour that the program lasted was an innovation Liberia will not soon forget. Some of the natives, who became convinced that the voice of Mr. Firestone actually did cross the sea, whis-

pered to one another of "the big boss man"
about whom they had heard so much and whose
voice came to them by a new kind of magic.
Though they might not understand his words,
every one of them grasped the spirit of good will
in his New Year's message.

Liberia having been joined to America by the
invisible bonds of radio, the farthest corners of
the country now are to be connected with the
seaboard. Firestone has begun the installation
of a wireless telephone system that will penetrate
to the jungle depths. The first station soon is to
begin operation at administrative headquarters
upon the Du, bringing that center into communication with Monrovia, the capital. Other
installations will follow, concentrating in a uni-
fied whole the Mount Barclay and Cavalla
plantations, the latter 250 miles from the Du, as
well as local points upon all of the plantations.

When opportunity permits it is planned to
extend this system into the deep bush, both for
the service of the Firestone organization and
missionary outposts. What a wireless telephone
somewhere nearby will signify in the solitary lives
of men marooned in the jungles of Liberia is not
easily imagined. The interior is as truly the dark
continent as it was half a century ago when
Stanley revealed unknown Africa. Missionaries
and educators who go among the tribes may not
visit Monrovia for a year at a time. Should an
emergency arise a week or two is likely to pass

before they learn the news. When a man in the hinterland starts for the coast he often must walk nine or ten days. But the nearest Firestone telephone station will bring the world to his door.

Chapter VII
THE CIVILIZING HAND AT WORK

Most of us think of Robinson Crusoe when we speak of the primitive. Robinson found about everything that a man could need upon his island and settled down to the simple life. While the tropics abound in luxuries these are not uniformly useful. Judged by the standards of civilization, a normal living is about as hard to get as anywhere else. The effort to establish a big organization in such a land was to produce unexpected results.

Medical service stands forth conspicuously. Soon after the first drive began the company brought over an American physician who established the foundation of a medical department. Starting with members of the staff this service gradually embraced the plantation workers, then the people of the country near by, until a large section of the population had fallen to Firestone's care.

Here in comfortable America it is hard to conceive of a country without a doctor in the interior and only one or two in the capital. An inevitable result was prevalence of disease, much of it preventable, which became the goal of Firestone medical service. When Justus B. Rice, Medical Officer, sat down to write his report of the half-year September 1, 1927, to February 29, 1928, he probably did not realize what an interesting job he would make of it. Reading Dr. Rice's report is like turning a telescope across the Atlantic. Moreover, he knew human nature as well as medicine.

"The half-year from September, 1927, to February, 1928, might be called the period of adolescence, characterized by further rapid growth and the beginnings of character," was his comment upon the medical department. "Just as during adolescence the child begins to look and act like a human being, so in this stage the department began to resemble a real medical department and to act like one.

"An interesting sidelight on the growth of the dispensary practice is the effect on the witch doctors. As far as healing the sick is concerned, the witches have been practically 'put out of business.' Hostile at first, they have come to regard the medical department as an ally rather than a rival. Two full-blown witches and one assistant witch have been treated in the hospital; and a number of others in the dispensary.

"More or less of a rogue's understanding has

been arrived at with these chaps. If they will cede all treatment of diseases to the medical department, the department in turn will not try to take over any of the other functions of a first class witch, such as the casting or removal of spells, causing the sun to shine or the rain to fall, etc. In fact, we deemed it wise to leave the control of the weather entirely in the hands of the witches. The witch doctors have lived up to their bargain, and even send patients in for treatment.

"The natives understand and appreciate the efforts of the medical department to an astonishing extent, especially when one considers their savage environment and past and utter newness of medical service to them. Sometimes this appreciation is expressed in a way very embarrassing to us—the kissing of hands and that sort of thing. More often, however, it is expressed in a desire to be of service. Convalescents consider it a great honor to be allowed to assist in the care of less fortunate patients. As often as not their efforts to assist hinder rather than help in the work, but the spirit is there."

Too bad to leave Dr. Rice and his witches, but it is necessary to hurry on and record that his infant medical department developed into a full grown hospital upon the Du plantation. There it came to be one of the marvels of Africa, an institution spreading its beneficent influence into the fastness of the jungle.

Ever since Firestone came to Liberia efforts have been under way to improve sanitation and health. Means were provided for an inquiry by the Harvard School of Tropical Medicine. Dr. Richard P. Strong of that institution led an expedition to the country made up of seven other specialists. They surveyed the medical, botanical and zoölogical phases of Liberian life, supplying the basis for organized scientific approach to the health problems of the country.

Their research was extended and applied under the direction of Dr. A. W. Sellards of the Harvard Medical School, who devoted special research to yellow fever and its prevention. By reason of experience elsewhere in the tropics Dr. Sellards was particularly qualified and his recommendations have had lasting results.

If the witch doctors leave a vivid impression, what shall be said of the leopard men? Any one peering into the jungle depths catches the sense of terror their name arouses. They are the supreme peril, the unfathomable horror. These leopard men make up a sinister voodoo society of the dark green world shut off from the rest of mankind. It must be true that their life among wild creatures, and maybe their own descent, has prompted the lust to stalk and slay like the leopard. It is not uncommon for some native wayfarer to be set upon along the trail and clawed into bits by the iron-hooked fingers of the leopard men. So compelling is their power

Former Jungle Land After the Fire and Ready for Planting

*A Medicine Man (above) and Two Devil Dancers
with Their Attendants (below)*

that a victim selected beforehand sometimes will go forth when his name is called in the night, knowing he never will return. Or one chief of the leopard men may say to another, "Last time it was a woman of my tribe; this time she must be of yours."

Dr. Strong noted, in his travels about the interior, that there were no cemeteries and few graves near some villages and he was informed recently buried corpses frequently were dug up for the leopard men's frenzies. Human bones could be seen at times, close to the trail. The leopard men are both killers and cannibals, whose weird beliefs hold that human flesh will make them powerful and thereby strengthen the power of their society.

From time to time the Liberian Government has endeavored to run down and exterminate the leopard men. Usually it is only by accident or revenge that one of the killers can be captured and punished. Nothing less than the infusion of civilization and a rigid enforcement agency will put an end to this organized system of voodoo.

While it need not cause surprise that the outside world knows little of Liberia, the plain truth is that Liberia knew little of its own territory and people until the coming of Firestone. When as many as 20,000 natives were brought together upon the plantations, the Firestone leaders realized that such a gathering presented unmatched opportunity to study native habits.

Again science was called in. George Schwab of
the Peabody Museum of Harvard University
undertook an anthropological and sociological
survey. His studies resulted in a history of native
life and customs that has gone far to provide
better understanding of the people.

Another effort of this character was directed
by G. Proctor Cooper III of the Yale School of
Forestry, dealing with the plant and wood life of
Liberia. Botanical and forest specimens were
sent to the Botanic Gardens in Kew, England,
and there identified, a valuable addition to
knowledge of the country. In recognition of
Firestone efforts the Yale School of Forestry has
bestowed the name of *Cassipourea Firestoneana*
upon one specimen of tree previously unidentified.

Encouragement of education holds a prominent place among the aims of Firestone. The
rubber men found that the natives rapidly
learned practical tasks. While it has not been
possible to achieve anything like ultimate goals
in the brief years since Firestone came, the company's trade school was a milestone. From the
foundation of the country American missionaries
had labored long and hard in Liberian school
rooms, but instruction in practical tasks was
developed only in recent years. The Booker T.
Washington Agricultural and Industrial Institute, modeled along the lines of the Hampton
and Tuskegee schools, is another cornerstone
of education for utility, as conducted by rep-

resentatives of American groups active in the country.

One of the abiding miracles of the rubber enterprise is the sight of a big American motor truck operated by a driver who never saw one until a few years ago. Even before the coming of Firestone a few natives had some mechanical knowledge, such as carpenters. Weighing the possibilities, the company sent an experienced teacher of carpentry and agriculture to Liberia. Tools were furnished, besides the instructor, and the carpentry course later progressed to furniture and cabinet making. Each student was paid a regular wage while acquiring technical knowledge which he in turn could impart to others.

Everywhere that the inquiring mind turns in Liberia there are curious contrasts, unexpected conditions. No less than twenty-seven dialects are spoken by the natives and it has been next to impossible for any white man to learn these tongues, because there were no written versions. Surely this was a strange situation—twenty-seven unrecorded tongues in so small a country.

Firestone has made it possible to reduce to writing and preserve the most commonly used dialect, the Kpelle language. As no books in the tongue existed the company supplied funds to compile a grammar, a most interesting educational enterprise carried out by Dr. Diedrich H. Westermann, noted German philologist.

English is the normal language of the coast and it has filtered into the bush during a hundred years of contact with traders. Any village will produce one or more spokesmen ready to palaver in pigeon English. Their own tongues consist almost wholly of phonetics and have an odd, hoarse sound to others. This bush English is a medley, reduced to the simplest terms and spoken without the usual connecting words.

But it is not without color. For instance, "small small" passes current when something is very small. "Softly softly" has the meaning of gently. "So so" bears exactly the same implication as in English, but the natives build up an effect by adding one of their hoarse terms, thus obtaining "So so wah-wah," which is very bad. This can be extended to "So so wah-wah me think," and so on.

Chapter VIII
TRANSFORMING THE PRIMITIVE

Everywhere Liberia was on the move. With the arrival of each ship came new equipment, conveniences and comforts. The outfitting and maintenance of such a large undertaking in a primitive country could be compared only to the upkeep of an army. A machine shop and commissary buildings were completed and a permanent warehouse established. Road building had begun, giving Liberians their first glimpse of American tractors, steam shovels and road rollers. Flimsily constructed bridges of trees and poles, regularly washed away during heavy rains, were solidly repaired and concrete bridges installed. For the first time in the memory of anybody the Government road was put in condition to be passable twelve months of the year. Within the two plantations other highways were opening the country. A real triumph of the construction program was a bridge 225 feet long, built of steel and concrete.

By the Fall of 1928 many miles of new highways were ready, afterward extended to a system embracing more than 100 miles. From a country practically without a road, Liberia rapidly went forward in the new day of transportation. The chugging of motors quickened the pulse of life in Monrovia. Trucks thundered through the streets, running from the waterside out to the plantation upon the Du. Wonder of wonders, Monrovia introduced traffic cops upon the principal corners.

With the growth of the Firestone technical staff the living problem also was intensified. Even at this early period a courageous wife or two from home came to live in the camps and more were to arrive. Akron heard persistent appeals for bath tubs. It might have been thought that men in the wilds would take to the nearest stream, but in Liberia such streams happen to be full of crocodiles and tiny organisms likely to cause fever.

The base back home shipped a consignment of bath tubs, which arrived in due season and were joyfully received. Whoever did not have a bath tub arranged to borrow his neighbor's, or the use of it. Both upon the Du and the Cavalla the supervisory staffs lived in towns of their own. Each community had a tank of purified water which served as the town reservoir. With the arrival of the bath tubs came piping to connect the houses to the reservoir, and another problem had been overcome.

In one way and another such was the adventure of hewing an empire from the jungle. When a saw mill, a radio plant and a bath tub could present formidable difficulties, each in a highly individual way, it may be understood how much trouble might arise from a misplaced tool at a critical moment. Or let us say that a bolt of a certain length and size should be missing, and not another of its dimensions in thousands of miles. Only the men who met and conquered these obstacles could tell the whole story.

Step by step the staff made livable homes in the jungle, or close to it. They were much the kind of homes that the same men would have lived in had they never left America. The social life of the camps, there at the edge of the wilds, was about what it would have been anywhere. The Saturday night bridge game developed into a fixed institution and the latest papers from home, although a month old, were read twice around.

Besides, there was a common responsibility that drew man to man. Every member of the staff felt himself studied by hundreds of observant eyes. Broadly speaking, the natives looked to the men above them with respect. But they probed them as well for those human weaknesses and foibles that mark men of all conditions. Long ago it was said that authority comes only from the ability to use it. By silent understanding everybody concerned knew that the white man in the black man's country had a position to maintain.

Previous to the Firestone era practically all the business of the country was carried on by the European traders and most of them charged the natives everything that the traffic would bear. Money earned upon the plantations rapidly was dissipated. Most of it went for nicknacks of one kind and another, the Liberians having a ready eye for adornment. Study indicated that it should be practical to import American merchandise at lower prices than the traders commonly charged. So it was only another step to Firestone's miniature department stores, upon the edge of the jungle, where almost any object may be bought from a safety pin to a motorcycle. The United States Trading Company, as this branch is known, took the further important step of establishing a banking department in Monrovia, upon the withdrawal of the Bank of British West Africa, Ltd., in October, 1930.

There were innumerable things to be done. The poultry of the country being scanty and of poor pedigree selected strains were introduced in an effort to improve the home stock. Then vegetable seeds and fruit trees were imported from America and model gardens laid out in an endeavor to teach better agriculture. Rice is the principal food of the country, with little variety of diet. Thus a better assortment of food becomes a part of the larger project to improve health.

As the needs of this pioneer life came to be

Harvey S. Firestone, Jr.   *...In the Rubber Plantations*

...With a Group of Native Workers

Modern Bungalow on the Firestone Plantations

better understood camp comforts increased until a man might have more than a fair dinner every night. Perhaps the greatest boon was the construction of two power plants, first upon the Du, then the Cavalla. The day that the current was turned on will not be readily forgotten in Liberia; certainly it will be kindly remembered by the rubber men. Those two power houses brought the triple blessings of electric light, power and refrigeration to a land where there had been only oil lamps, man power and heat. It was something of an experience to open the door of a refrigerator and find a cold drink inside.

The moment that the power plants were brought into service it was possible to use the current for tasks previously performed by hand or left in abeyance until the power came. Mechanical operations of every kind gained headway. High tension lines were run for miles across the plantations and suitable connections made wherever power might be required. Gradually the big enterprise was transformed.

While so much was being done to improve working and living conditions for the white man, the native did not lack attention. Plans were laid to improve his villages wherever possible without affecting his contentment. Using the ordinary village as a type Firestone engineers determined as a principle to induce better sanitation and improve the native house as experience might indicate. For one thing, it was planned to build model villages provided with running water, shower baths and similar facilities. Each village would have a large and pleasant park and playground in the center, with free movies now and then.

In order to obtain a permanent record of this changing world a motion picture expedition sponsored by the company has photographed the country and its people, along with its new industry. The film is an educational record of the first order and a rare treat as well.

It has been shown extensively throughout the United States and wherever exhibited never fails to attract interest. Educators and students have followed its moving panorama as a living record. But no one has taken a livelier interest in the Liberian films than the Liberian natives have shown in American films. At the first sight of the New York skyline many of them took to the jungle. Hitherto their conception of height had been limited by the tallest tree they ever saw. Most of them never have accepted the "mountain buildings" as real, but rather a bit of false magic, because downright, genuine magic can be depended upon and the white men's "ju ju" is doubtful.

Looked at from any standpoint substantial progress marked the year of 1928 and this progress was to broaden upon an expanding scale in the years to come. The working force, native and American, had grown until approximately 20,000 men labored for the modern needs of civilization. The planted areas made up 15,000 acres by the end of '28 and the years that followed were to see upward of 10,000,000 rubber trees growing upon 55,000 acres of retrieved jungle. Problems that once seemed almost past solution had been overcome and the dilemmas of yesterday turned into the accomplished facts of today. The new Liberia stirred with activity and enterprise, with life and hope.

Chapter IX

THE DARK SHADOW

Americans think of slavery as a melancholy memory belonging to some distant time which it is as well not to recall—the dark age of man. Yet slavery endures to this day in Africa, Asia and other corners of the world. If not actual slavery of the market place and the auction block, then a condition so little removed that the difference lies in name only.

Hardly more than a dozen years ago a new moral force appeared in the world known as the League of Nations. No matter if it has not been powerful enough to grapple with all of the world's problems, the League has come to be regarded as an agency of justice between nations. One of the special charges given to a section of the League is the searching out and uprooting of slavery, under any guise. It is permanently engaged in discovering and exterminating this evil by every means at its command.

Despite American impressions to the contrary, slavery in Africa is inherent and about as difficult to control as prohibition enforcement ever was in America; a fact that must be borne patiently in mind to understand African life.

Liberia has not escaped the taint. From the foundation of the Republic, and before, there was slavery or near slavery and these conditions have persisted to the present day. Until twenty-five years ago the Liberian Government had very little control over the interior, or its population of more than one and a half millions of people. This hinterland is one of the densely populated areas of the continent; therefore a fertile ground for slavery.

In the Spring of 1929 an American clergyman traveling in African waters observed a number of Liberian "boys" herded together upon his ship, bound for Fernando Po, a Spanish island not far off shore. Probably their unhappy look caused him to investigate. He learned that they were "contract laborers," the contract being in favor of those who sent them and those who employed them; a disguise so slight as to be easily penetrated by the minister's eyes.

He returned to America and protested to Washington. Sometimes one man's word is a powerful thing and so it proved in this case. As when a pebble is dropped into placid water, the ripple spread, touching far shores. Before long the effects were noted in London, Paris and

Geneva—especially Geneva, home of the League.
These multiplied results found expression in a
note handed to the Liberian Secretary of State,
June 8, 1929, by the American Chargé d'Affaires:

"I am directed by the Secretary of State to advise Your Excellency that there have come to
the attention of the Government of the United
States from several sources reports bearing reliable evidence of authenticity which definitely
indicate that existing conditions incident to the
so-called 'export' of labor from Liberia to Fernando Po have resulted in the development of a
system which seems hardly distinguishable from
organized slave trade, and that in the enforcement of this system the services of the Liberian
Frontier Force, and the services and influences
of certain high Government officials are constantly and systematically used."

Upon receipt of such a challenge any Government must have taken prompt action. Three
days later the Secretary of State made a "cate-
gorical denial," declaring that the ". . . Government of the Republic will have no objection to
this question being investigated on the spot by a
competent, impartial and unprejudiced commission."

The permanent delegate of Liberia to the
League next addressed a communication to the
Council of that body, charging that the country
was an object of propaganda, also inviting the
Council to name a commission. The Council re-

sponded by selecting Dr. Cuthbert Christy of England as its representative, the United States named Dr. Charles S. Johnson, a Negro educator, and Liberia appointed Arthur Barclay, a former President of the country. This group was officially received by President King as the League's International Commission of Enquiry and the "Christy Commission," as it came to be known, was active in Liberia for a number of weeks, conducting hearings and investigating conditions.

The sum total of its findings was handed to the League, September 8, 1930, and must stand for a long while as an example of impartial inquiry, the report opening pages of contemporary history never scanned before. This report is available at the Government Printing Office in Washington and worthy of reading.*

Upon authority of the commission it was stated that the Liberian population of American extraction numbers no more than 10,000 and constitutes a governing class. The natives as a whole have no voice in the Government, the voting franchise being restricted to the Liberians and a few natives admitted to this class.

Proceeding directly to the question of slavery, the commission found that captives taken in wars between tribes made up a numerous group held in bondage ". . . and many of them continue

*Report of theInternational Commission of Enquiry into the Existence of Slavery and Forced Labor in the Republic of Liberia. Department of State Publication No. 147, 1931.

in their status as captive slaves." The common-
place system of pawning children, relatives,
slaves already held captive, and any other chance
human property, served to maintain a still
larger class, according to the commission. Evi-
dently any head of a family might pawn those
under his control, as a chief could dispose of a
member of his tribe. The prevailing price advanced for women left as pawns was placed at
£6 and for men £4.

The commission pointed out that it had no
evidence to prove the existence of slave trading
or slave holding ". . . by Americo-Liberians in
the classic sense, involving all the rights of owner-
ship, but there is evidence that they have taken
natives as pawns." Although a President of
Liberia decreed in 1923 that ". . . pawns may
redeem themselves" the commission found that
"In practice it is impossible for a person pawned
to redeem himself." Furthermore, it was shown
that any person with sufficient power not only
may pawn another, but the human pledge then
may be repawned to a third person. Should such
pawn run away, it has been ruled by a Liberian
court that a shilling a day may be added to the
debt during his absence.

Back of this shadow falls another of yet darker
hue. It was freely testified before the commission
that excessive fines have been imposed by the
Government for failure to do "road work" and
similar tasks. When they failed to pay, witnesses

said, their villages were raided, sometimes burned, and men and women flogged. The Liberian Frontier Force repeatedly was named in this connection. Witnesses pleading in their own behalf stated that they had been compelled to pawn members of their families and tribes in order to pay these excessive fines. Two instances of the testimony will suffice, from page 21 of the report as published in Washington:

"Varnai Quai, a headman from Baimeh, fined for road delinquencies and for failure to provide carriers, £17.5.0, pawned two sons for £8 and £7 respectively to one Karpali in Weijo two years ago without much prospect of redemption."

"Jallah, of Teh section, fined £5 for road delinquencies, pawned his son to one Mr. Law, an Americo-Liberian, for £5 two years and four months from April 21, 1930. The boy ran away after four months and court costs for returning him increased his redemption fee by £7.13.0. For each day the boy was away the court decided he had to pay to the holder one shilling."

Besides these practices the commission ruled that contract laborers ". . . shipped to Fernando Po and French Gabun from the southern counties of Liberia have been recruited under conditions of criminal compulsion scarcely distinguishable from slave raiding and slave trading." The commission charged Vice-President Allen Yancey of Liberia and other officials with complicity and

with use of the armed Liberian Frontier Force
to carry out these plans.

No sooner was the Christy report filed than
the former ripple became a wave of protest.
Upon November 5, 1930, the United States
Government notified Liberia that this country
was "profoundly shocked." World pressure
settled about the Negro Republic. President
King resigned, December 2, 1930, and Edwin J.
Barclay succeeded to the office. By December 19
the British Government asked that the Liberian
matter be placed upon the League agenda for
the January Council meeting. The 19th day of
that month, in 1931, religious and philanthropic
groups composing the American Advisory Committee on Education in Liberia, met in New York
and pledged support to the United States.

Swiftly the Liberian question passed from the
stage of a minor African problem into a world
issue. Liberia took the next step, asserting in-
ability to carry out recommendations of the commission because it lacked the necessary funds.
Hence the League set up a special sub-committee
to consider ways and means. The American
Government named to this commission our
Chargé d'Affaires in Monrovia, Samuel Reber, Jr.
Sessions were held in London and the new
sub-committee next appointed a group of administrative experts to visit Liberia, consisting
of Messrs Brunot, Ligthart and Mackenzie.
They arrived in June of 1931. Their efforts re-

sulted in the formulation of a plan of assistance presented to the League of Nations and discussed elsewhere in these pages.

The chaotic condition of Liberian affairs took another turn when the Foreign Office in London instructed Constantine Graham, its Chargé d'Affaires in Monrovia, to protest against the treatment of the Kru tribes. For months there had been evidence of stringent measures employed by the Liberian Government in dealing with this group of natives. Sir John Simon, Secretary of State for Foreign Affairs, cabled the British representative to obtain the co-operation of the resident French and American diplomats, if possible, but otherwise to protest alone within a fortnight. His instructions of February 18, 1932, read in part:

"His Majesty's Government in the United Kingdom are satisfied that the proceedings of the Liberian Frontier Force under Colonel [T. Elwood] Davis in the Kru country last Autumn were tyrannical and highhanded in an inexplicable degree.

"According to information which His Majesty's Government cannot disregard, although they equally cannot as yet regard it as confirmed, these proceedings are being repeated at the present time and are exposing Kru population to personal violence and outrage and the destruction of property.

"... His Majesty's Government must, however, irrespective of motives underlying measures which have been taken against Krus, ask for an explicit assurance that such proceedings will be discontinued immediately pending conclusion of an arrangement between the League, United States of America and Liberia for future administration of the country."

To this demand the Monrovian Government replied that as the charges were unfounded and unconfirmed in the eyes of the British Foreign Office, then ". . . the question of an explicit assurance that such action should cease does not arise."

The French, German and American Governments had concurred in the demand and the Liberian reply failed to satisfy any of the four nations concerned in the protest.

A statement that may be said fairly to sum up the international viewpoint was reported in the Parliamentary Debates of the House of Lords for March 16, 1932. Viscount Snowden, the Lord Privy Seal, spoke as follows:

". . . The noble Earl, Lord Buxton, asked if I could state what was the attitude of the Government at present in regard to diplomatic relations with Liberia. In concert with the Government of the United States, His Majesty's Government decided to withhold recognition of Mr. Barclay's administration until it had given satisfactory evidence of a desire to act upon the recommendations of the International Commission, and

the position at the moment is that His Majesty
has no representative in the capital. The Chargé
d'Affaires is not fully accredited, because subsequent events have not, in the opinion of His
Majesty's Government, justified him in present-
ing his credentials to the Government. That is
the position in regard to the diplomatic relations
of His Majesty's Government with Liberia at the
present time.

". . . The French and American Governments
agreed to coöperate with His Majesty's Government in taking this step, and the representatives
of the three powers . . . had an interview with
President Barclay last week, on March 7. The
next day the reply of the Liberian Government
was received, which, I am afraid, I can hardly
describe to your Lordships as being of a very
satisfactory or conciliatory character . . ."

As the next development and at the suggestion
of the British Foreign Office, it was decided to
send an investigator into the Kru country who
might report his own impartial observations.
D. G. Rydings, British Vice-Consul in Monrovia, was the man selected. Leaving the capital
March 14 he proceeded by ship to the Kru
coast and there undertook a survey graphically
reported in an official document which he handed
to Mr. Graham bearing date of April 15, 1932.

After describing his entrance into the country
and mode of travel and the welcome extended to
him, he noted that the natives were loath to

discuss their troubles, in fear of reprisals. A center of disturbance proved to be the town of Nana Kru, where the paramount chief had been elevated to that position by Colonel Davis, against the wishes of the tribesmen, or most of them. They expelled the spurious chief, Pyne Nyekan, and he resorted to the Liberian Frontier Force, which invaded the country.

". . . On their arrival a number of prominent tribesmen and their wives were immediately put in chains and imprisoned," wrote Mr. Rydings. "Women were raped by the soldiers without any intervention by the officials, and men who had been taken prisoners were severely beaten."

Afterward another chief was elected, more acceptable to the tribe, but he was prevented from exercising his authority and Pyne Nyekan ruled in his stead as "acting" paramount chief, which increased tribal bitterness.

The trend of Liberian military methods may be judged from another passage of the Rydings report: "I am informed that when Colonel Davis arrived at Nana Kru in August, 1931, with a force of about 200 of his soldiers, he caused the arrest of some fifty natives on charges of seditious propaganda, and confined them in the custom house until he left Nana Kru in November in order to proceed to Sasstown. This seditious propaganda consisted in a tendency to discuss the possible intervention of the League of Nations in the administration of Liberia and openly to express preference for white rule. Natives who gave expression to such views were considered to be guilty of seditious practices."

Several tribes had deserted their villages, or what remained of them, and retreated to the dense bush, where they might be out of reach. The British Vice-Consul was a man of spirit. Not content that his investigation should be restricted to territory controlled by the Liberian Frontier Force he proposed that its officers assist him to visit the hinterland. Instead, they put one obstacle after another in his way. But he established contact with the vanquished tribes and penetrated to their new retreats, where he found them in much distress.

A typical illustration of the treatment they had received was summed up in the following words of his report: "The plantation town of Wolokri in the Sasstown interior was attacked in the night when the inhabitants were asleep and totally unprepared. The soldiers crept into the banana plantations, which surround all native villages, and poured volleys into the huts. In the subsequent confusion and flight women and children were ruthlessly shot down and killed. One woman who had that day been delivered of twins was shot in her bed, and the infants perished in the flames when the village was fired by the troops. At this town three men, fourteen women and eight children met their death.

"The whole of the Sasstown area has been laid waste and every town, with the exception of New Sasstown, has been burnt and pillaged by the Liberian Frontier Force. Nothing remains of what were previously prosperous villages but a few charred posts, ashes and broken utensils. Clothing, personal effects and stocks of rice (the principal article of diet of the natives) were destroyed in the flames or pillaged by soldiers, and cattle, goats and poultry killed by the troops for their consumption.

". . . Some 12,000 natives, who have been harried and subjected to punitive raids for months past, have taken refuge in the bush, where they are suffering from exposure and malnutrition and are existing under conditions of extreme hardship."

Other examples of brutality, pillaging and destruction were available upon every hand, as the Vice-Consul pointed out, his conclusion being that the Kru people had suffered inhuman treatment. His report was transmitted to the Foreign Office in London, there to become a basis of the case against the Liberian Government.

Up to the day of publication there is no evidence to show that the conditions brought to light have been altered.

There the matter has rested, at least as far as Liberia is concerned.

Chapter X
THE PLAN OF ASSISTANCE

LIBERIAN governmental difficulties have been steadily aggravated by reason of persistent opposition to reform. As early as 1930* the Finance Corporation of America withheld further advances under the loan agreement because the Liberian Government failed to comply with its contract. Specific charges were filed that budget requirements were not being met; that the Government had failed to compel the payment of consular fees and taxes, or to punish officials for embezzlement of public funds. Numerous other infractions were cited and a proper accounting asked. These protests having no effect, the Finance Corporation declined to pay subsequent installments of the loan. Sinking fund and interest payments fell into default in January and July of 1932.

Turning the pages of the record it becomes

*See Appendix, pages 178-181.

possible to see how the Republic steadily en-
tangled itself, step by step. Upon April 29, 1932,
the Financial Adviser called to the President's
attention that revenues were less than expenses
and predicted floating indebtedness would reach
$700,000 by the end of the year.

One fact emerged clearly from these and
successive developments. Liberia could not settle
her troubles within any reasonable time, except
by outside help, because her troubles long since
passed the scope of her capacity. Meanwhile the
problems of law enforcement, sanitation and
proper conduct of the government pressed for
solution.*

During the Summer of 1932 conditions drifted
in the same direction. Toward the end of June
Dr. M. D. Mackenzie again arrived in Liberia
upon a mission for the League, delegated as special commissioner to mediate among warring Kru
tribes. His coming proved an event of public interest but looked upon with doubtful sentiments.
Liberians observed that Dr. Mackenzie arrived
aboard the English gunboat *Rochester*, accompanied by an armed escort of one non-commis-
sioned officer from a Gold Coast regiment and
four native policemen. Since the presence in a
friendly country of armed forces belonging to
another nation would be thought extraordinary
anywhere, the incident was regarded as an ominous sign.

*See Appendix, pages 171 and 190.

Public uncertainty and growing discontent reached such a state of anxiety that, upon August 11, the Liberian Legislature revived and amended a Sedition Act under the terms of which any one opposing the Government or speaking critically of the President might be imprisoned from three to seven years and have his property confiscated.

This legislation effectually silenced citizens of the country, but it did not check the trend of events. Again, the 17th of December, the Legislature passed an Act which, in effect, repudiated the loan agreement. Upon the 23rd it was approved by President Barclay. The American State Department protested this decision, without result. A few days later the Liberian House of Representatives adopted a Resolution of condemnation directed at P. J. Fitzsimmons, Acting Financial Adviser, because of his objections to repudiation. The Legislature next enacted that the floating debt be funded in twenty-year three per cent. bonds, contrary to the loan agreement.

But all recognition of contracts by Liberian officials was not yet at an end. The 27th of December R. Emmons Dixon, Attorney-General, was reported to have advised the President and Cabinet that the repudiation legislation of December 17 was unconstitutional. F. E. R. Johnson, Chief Justice of the Supreme Court, took the same position. Such a resolute stand by these two men might have been expected to bring about a reversal of the earlier legislative action, but officials in control persistently refused to observe the loan contract.

Neither the League nor the United States could stand aside while international relations were flaunted so recklessly. President Hoover, after consultation with Mr. Roosevelt, then the President-elect, designated Major-General Blanton Winship as Representative of the President of the United States on Special Mission to Liberia. The 28th of February, 1933, the State Department announced:

"Believing that the acceptance by Liberia of international assistance looking toward the reorganization of Liberian administration offered the best guarantee of needed social reforms, the American Government has participated in the work of the Liberian Committee of the League of Nations at Geneva. The American Government last October endorsed the program elaborated by the Liberian Committee, and forwarded it to the Firestone interests as a basis for certain modifications in the contract between them and Liberia.

"The progress toward the rehabilitation of Liberian finances and a sounder general understanding between this country and Liberia has been blocked by a series of recent occurrences and it is clear that a reëxamination by a special American representative on the ground is neces-

Typical Worker Tapping a Rubber Tree

Native Houses and a New Home That Soon Will Be Ready

sary. . . . The special representative is being sent
to Monrovia in an effort to provide a solution
safeguarding American rights in Liberia and
restoring at the same time a situation which will
permit of further efforts to assist Liberia."

Since the visit of the League experts in 1931
attempts had been made by the League to put
into effect a plan of assistance, but to no avail.
The fact had become increasingly evident that
any plan of assistance must be founded upon a
suitable financial basis. By invitation of the
League Liberian Committee, Harvey S. Firestone, Jr., attended its meetings in Geneva and
London during May and June of 1933.* The
extent of the company's interests in Liberia
prompted the League committee to inquire if
Firestone would underwrite the cost of applying
the plan of assistance evolved by the League
committee. In connection with this plan it was
definitely noted that, "The members of the committee other than the Liberian representative
are in full agreement with the recommendations
of its financial expert and approve his proposals.
Under the present circumstances these appear
to them to be the best solution for promoting the
development of Liberia. The Liberian representative put in a memorandum . . . making
certain reservations."

Mr. Firestone, Jr., told the committee that he
recognized the difficulties of Liberia and the Gov-

*See Appendix, page 179.

ernment and looked with sympathy upon the League's efforts to assist. As a means of putting into practice the findings and recommendations of the committee, the Finance Corporation of America would relax the terms of the loan contract, a concession received by the committee as practical and satisfactory evidence of Firestone coöperation.

Mr. Firestone, Jr., agreed permanently to reduce interest charges from seven to five per cent. upon the loan held by the Finance Corporation. Although the former rate prevailed for foreign loans placed in the United States at the time of the Liberian loan, he made the offer in the light of present circumstances. The saving to Liberia by this reduction of interest rate, together with the contemplated reduction in salaries of fiscal officers under the loan agreement, would approximate $62,000 annually.

Anticipating that the Liberian Government might not be able to pay even this reduced rate of interest, Mr. Firestone, Jr., renounced the right to interest payments in such years as current revenues were less than $502,000, estimated as necessary for the operating expenses of the Government and the cost of the plan of assistance. This concession might amount to $125,000 a year.

The basis of assistance then decided upon by the committee was the appointment of a supervisory staff of nine members to represent the

League in Liberia, these agents having authority to help administer the law, improve sanitation and otherwise coöperate with the Government. A Chief Adviser was to direct this staff, at a total estimated cost of $78,000 a year for salaries.

The League committee showed anxiety to obtain assurance of proper maintenance for its staff. At this point the Finance Corporation offered to set up a working capital of $150,000 for Liberia, guaranteeing that the fund should be sufficient to pay salaries and expenses of the staff at all times.

Liberia, upon its part, would accept and approve by legislative action the proposed supplementary agreement to the original loan agreement, and rescind any laws or orders which contravened these agreements. Such action, of course, would annul the repudiation Act of 1932. Also by legislative action Liberia must ratify the League plan of assistance. Furthermore, the Government would resume the deposit of Government funds with the depository officially designated to receive such monies, but which were now withdrawn. Lastly, Liberia would agree to pay off gradually the internal floating debt without the issuance of three per cent. bonds.

Such was the plan of assistance as it stood upon June 27, 1933, worked out by the League after two or more years of extensive research and hearings and in conformity with the advice of its experts as well as the best opinion of the committee. Among the exceptions then registered the Liberian delegate, Louis A. Grimes, Secretary of State, said that ". . . Mr. Firestone has conditioned his coöperation with the plan on the appointment of an American citizen as Chief Adviser; but inasmuch as by the terms of the loan contract the Financial Adviser will be a citizen of America, and one of the principal duties of the Chief Adviser will be to arbitrate between the Government of Liberia and the Financial Adviser in case of a dispute, it does not appear to the Liberian delegation that such an appointment would inspire in the rank and file of Liberian citizens that confidence necessary to ensure belief and trust in the impartiality of his decisions, nor that the League was being adequately represented by having as its principal Officier du Liaison a citizen of a non-member state."

This stand was not the viewpoint of the Federal Council of the Churches of Christ in America, nor of the American Advisory Committee on Education in Liberia, representing other well known organizations which have extended assistance to the people of Liberia over a period of years. The first named body made representations to the American Government, in the course of which it was emphasized that, "The executive committee of the Federal Council of the Churches of Christ in America desires to express to the Department of State its earnest hope that the Chief Adviser of the Liberian Government, proposed in the League of Nations' plan, shall be an American citizen, familiar with the history of Liberia and sympathetic with the educational, missionary and racial interest of large American groups in the people of that land. The basis for this hope is due to the fact that the United States has maintained for many long years an attitude of altruistic friendship for Liberia, far exceeding in quality and extent that of any other nation. The Government and people of the United States have, we believe, a definite and unique contribution to make to the advancement of Liberia and Liberians, a contribution which has vital significance also for the whole continent of Africa."

The sentiments expressed by Mr. Grimes before the League committee were not the sentiments of the Liberian people and Senate as stated no longer ago than the previous August, in an official letter of "advice" from the Senate to the President. It was then said, "That in notifying Liberia's acceptance of said plan of assistance, the President, should the diplomatic situation be favorable, shall indicate to the Council of the League of Nations the Government of Liberia's desire that the Chief Adviser, to be appointed by the League of Nations under said plan of assistance, shall be an American citizen of requisite competency, recommended by the President of the United States of America, and acceptable to the President of Liberia."

The Liberian Government was requested to ratify or reject the League plan before the meeting of the Council of the League should take place in September, 1933. Under date of August 25, the British and American Governments handed a joint note to Liberia saying that ". . . the present plan of assistance provides an opportunity which they are informed is not likely to recur for Liberia to obtain the assistance which she has requested from the League of Nations. They consider that the present proposals will provide a solution of the problems confronting Liberia.

"Upon the acceptance by Liberia of these proposals and the extension, when the plan becomes operative, of an amnesty to all political prisoners detained, His Britannic Majesty's Government and the Government of the United States of America will be prepared to recognize and to enter into full diplomatic relations with the existing Liberian administration."

Three days later Liberia acknowledged this joint communication, promising consideration in time for the Council meeting. Afterward Liberia assumed the position that as the plan of assistance had been recommended by a committee of the League, and not by the Council itself, the Liberian Government declined to take any formal action regarding the plan until the Council had passed upon it.

The 6th day of September the Government

filed representations with the League against the appointment of an American as Chief Adviser, and these objections were so framed that they likewise would apply to a British or French citizen, which brought events to another pause.

Chapter XI
INTERNATIONAL AID BLOCKED

Negotiations had reached a stalemate when the Council met early in October of 1933. General Winship, the American representative, promptly took up the question of the Chief Adviser. Speaking before the committee upon the 9th day of the month, he said:*

"The American Government has not heretofore expressed itself before the committee on the question of the nationality of the Chief Adviser to Liberia under the proposed League plan of assistance. It has been the personal view of the American representative that what was needed was a man of outstanding character, competence and ability, irrespective of his nationality, but that a Chief Adviser of American nationality might be especially desirable from the point of view of Liberia, in that his presence might promote an increase in contributions by various

*See Appendix, page 142.

interested organizations in the United States for educational, religious and medical purposes.

"The American Government is aware that there have been objections in certain quarters to an American Chief Adviser. It believes that it is of vital importance that a plan of assistance to Liberia should be established without delay. The American Government does not maintain that the Chief Adviser should be of American nationality."

General Winship then proceeded to discuss the objections raised by Mr. Grimes.

". . . Mr. Grimes' main contentions," said General Winship, "are as follows:

"1. That in 1926 Liberia 'did not desire a loan, either for financial or economic rehabilitation, or any other existing necessity' . . . but that its 'reluctant' acceptance was forced on Liberia by Firestone interests.

"2. That 'a large proportion of the amount of the loan was misspent and even thrown away, without any benefit to Liberia. . . .'

"3. That the present economic condition of Liberia is due to the existence of the Finance Corporation loan of 1926 and to the bad judgment and incompetence of the advisership officials appointed thereunder.

"The American representative has carefully examined the statements made or sponsored by Mr. Grimes, and in many instances he has been able to check his allegations with the original

records. The American representative finds Mr.
Grimes' statements inaccurate and misleading,
and his conclusions without foundation. A detailed statement* in connection with Mr. Grimes'
contentions is being submitted for the information of the committee. It is shown therein:

"1. That Liberia sought the Finance Corporation loan for the following reasons:

"a. In order to liquidate the internal and
floating debts, which had risen to over
$600,000, and

"b. In order to relieve Liberia of the Customs receivership established under the
1912 loan.

"Both of these objectives were realized under
the Finance Corporation loan agreement.

"The American Government concerned itself
in the loan to the extent of extending good offices
during preliminary discussions, and of intimating
that, should Liberia so request, the American
Government would be willing to assume certain
clearly defined functions with respect to arbitration and the designation of loan officials. The
American Government did not induce American
capital to invest in the loan, nor did it assume
responsibility for its security.

"2. Over ninety per cent. of the proceeds of
the bonds issued under the Finance Corporation
loan went to retire prior obligations of Liberia.
That less than ten per cent. was utilized for other

*See Appendix, pages 165–179.

purposes, was due to Liberia's early violations of the loan agreement and to the refusal of the Liberian Government satisfactorily to settle these matters. Had they been settled, further funds would have been made available for general purposes.

"Mr. [Sidney] De La Rue, first Financial Adviser under the loan, had to do with the expenditure of only approximately $50,000 from loan funds, and not $156,000 as alleged in a Liberian statement. The question of Mr. De La Rue's judgment in this matter is one of opinion.

"The foreign officials serving Liberia under the Finance Corporation loan agreement have been men of character, experience and proven ability. They have given the Liberian Government constructive advice on repeated occasions. Among other matters, they have advised the Liberian Government regarding:

"Waste of public funds in the maintenance of overstaffed or unnecessary institutions and bureaus; failure of the Government to enforce the payment of delinquent taxes; failure of the Government to prosecute Liberian officials for embezzlement, or to take action against them under their bonds; failure of the Government to enforce the payment into the Treasury of consular and other fees; failure of the Government to foster or encourage commerce, or to open the hinterland to trade; failure of the Government to interest itself in the condition of

38449

the million and a half native peoples, or to utilize the taxes collected from the natives for their benefit.*

"The advice and recommendations of the foreign officials appointed under the Finance Corporation loan agreement have been met with opposition or indifference on the part of the Liberian Government. The failure of the Government to act is responsible for the conditions which exist in Liberia at present.

"The unwillingness of the Liberian Government to accept competent advice has not been confined to the relations of the Government with the various American advisers appointed under the loan agreement, or previously. The majority of the recommendations of the 1930 commission of inquiry do not appear to have been put into effect, and the recommendations made to Liberia by the experts appointed under the auspices of the League of Nations since 1931, have been opposed."

The position of the American Government being established, General Winship analyzed Liberian affairs in further detail.

"The Firestone interests recommended the acceptance of a loan by Liberia," he said. "They were of the opinion that the proceeds of a loan, if utilized in the proper way, would promote the general development of the country and in this sense contribute to the successful prosecution of

*See Appendix, page 190.

the company's main interest,—the plantation project. There is likewise evidence that Mr. Firestone shared the widespread American interest in the progress of Liberia, and that, entirely aside from his business concerns, he wished to see the country develop along sound economic and social lines. There is no evidence that, when the matter of a Liberian loan was first considered, the Firestone organization itself had any interest in financing such an issue. The Firestone Company desired, on the contrary, that such a loan should be made by the American Government, and included a paragraph (k) in the original draft of the plantation agreement to this effect.

"This draft was submitted to the Secretary of State (Mr. Hughes) in a letter from Mr. Firestone dated December 10, 1924. Mr. Hughes replied, under date of December 22, 1924, stating (with reference to paragraph k) that:

"'In this connection, it should be clearly understood that this statement in the contract . . . must not be taken by the Government of Liberia or in any other quarter to mean that I intend to reopen the question of a Government loan or that any committal in this respect is involved.'"

Continuing, General Winship said: "The American Government neither induced American capital to invest in the loan, nor did it assume responsibility for its security. This was recog-

nized by President King at the time and on
October 28, 1928, he referred to the loan in the
following terms:

"'It has also been suggested that the Liberian
Government was coerced by the United States
Department of State in making the Firestone
rubber agreement and the obtaining of the seven
per cent. gold loan of 1927. . . .

"'Knowing these charges to be absolutely untrue, I felt it a duty we owe not only to the
United States Government but to ourselves to
make a public denial of them.

"'The presence of American assistance to the
financial administration of Liberian affairs was
not unsolicited, but rather a realization of the
desires of the people of Liberia . . .

"'The American Government during the
whole period of its unbroken friendly intercourse
with Liberia, has never sought any special
political right or economic privilege for itself or
its citizens; but rather, has always stood four
square in the "open door policy" of equal opportunity and equal treatment by Liberia to all
foreign nations.'"

General Winship having concluded, Mr. Grimes
again reviewed his objections at length, which
prompted Viscount Cecil, chairman of the committee, to say, as noted in the minutes:

". . . that the interplay of proposals and coun-
ter proposals which had already been going on
for two years could not be allowed to continue

indefinitely. The time would come—and personally he thought it had come now—to ask the
Liberian Government to state quite plainly
whether it accepted or rejected the plan. It was
impossible to allow the matter to drag on indefinitely without any final decision. The situation was becoming detrimental to the Liberian
Government, to the Liberian people and to the
League itself. He trusted that by the end of this
session the committee would have received a
final affirmative or negative reply from the Liberian Government, leaving nothing more in
doubt."

Thus admonished, the Liberian delegation submitted detailed reservations and amendments,
contending that the minimum budget figure of
$300,000 should be increased to $375,000, and
the $150,000 allotted to the plan of assistance be
reduced. At the suggestion of Mr. Firestone,
through his representative, the minimum budget
was increased to $325,000 in order to provide
an additional $25,000 for education. The League
committee maintained that $150,000 would not
be excessive in carrying out the plan of assistance.

When the amended plan was brought before
the Council, the 14th of October, Viscount Cecil
announced that he was advised the Finance
Corporation of America stood ready to accept
the plan as revised and assume the obligations
imposed. This announcement also made known

that in order to remove the obstacles raised by the Liberian position regarding the nationality of the Chief Adviser, Firestone now conceded this vital point, formerly regarded as indispensable.

Mr. Grimes persisting in his objections to many provisions of the plan which he said might infringe upon the Constitution and the sovereignty of the country, Viscount Cecil reminded him that Liberia had applied to the League for assistance and was at liberty to refuse the offer about to be made. But, he added, ". . . it was the opinion of the committee, an opinion which he believed to be well founded, that unless something of the kind was done the political independence of Liberia would be in serious danger."

Salvador de Madariaga, the representative of Spain, made an attempt to reconcile all parties, saying he was convinced that much benefit would be derived from adoption of the plan. He took occasion to emphasize that as he had been ". . . among those who had most clearly drawn the Council's attention to these difficulties, he was in duty bound to lay stress on the really important concessions which the enterprise in question (Firestone) had made in order to facilitate the committee's task. . . . He was convinced that, as was proved by the generous concessions to which he had just alluded and on which he wished to lay special emphasis, the Firestone Company would be on the Council's side. . . . If the Liberian

*The Day's Harvest of Rubber Latex Comes
into the Collection Depot*

Waiting for the Payroll, the Only One in Liberia

Republic would help them, it would find the Council by its side."

Whereupon the committee report, embracing the plan of assistance as a protocol,* was unanimously adopted by the Council, the Liberian representative abstaining from voting. The next necessary action became adoption or rejection by Liberia.

Anticipating a prompt decision, the United States Department of State announced publicly, the 19th of November, 1933:

"The American Government expects Liberia to accept the plan of assistance and will be pleased in this case to coöperate in its successful execution. Should the present administration at Monrovia reject this opportunity, such action could only be construed as opposition to reforms the urgent desirability of which has been apparent for over three years, and as indifference to the welfare of the million and a half native peoples of Liberia."

At last the long-drawn negotiations apparently drew near to a conclusion advantageous to everybody. But this expectation was not to be realized. After prolonged discussion the two houses of the Liberian Legislature framed a joint resolution upon January 12, 1934, which set forth "That the President of Liberia be hereby authorized to accept on behalf of the Government of the Republic of Liberia in principle the basis outlined

*See Appendix, pages 134–160.

in the said Proposed Plan of Assistance laid down in the protocol, with the following exceptions. . . ."

These reservations were substantially the same as those which the League previously had considered at length. Consequently, further insistence upon these points amounted to rejection by the Liberian Government, in view of the definite League stand that the plan must be accepted as a whole.

Four days after the resolution was drawn and communicated to the League Council in Geneva, that body received a statement from the representative of Poland, Count E. Raczynski, the official Rapporteur of the Council. He reviewed the negotiations with Liberia, observing: "My colleagues will in this connection note that the committee stated in its report that the present plan represents the considered conditions upon which assistance could, in the opinion of the committee, be granted to Liberia, and that the plan as it stands must be taken as a whole. . . ."

The Polish representative further noted that Viscount Cecil had said:

"If the Liberian Government should be so ill-advised as not to carry out the scheme in its entirety, then the only consequence would be that the scheme would come to an end and the Liberian Government would again be in the position that it occupies at the present moment."

Proceeding, the Rapporteur pointed out:

"We have now received the reply of the Liberian Government, forwarded to the Secretary-General by the permanent representative of Liberia at Geneva, in a letter dated January 13, 1934. This begins by announcing that:

"'The Legislature of Liberia has authorized the acceptance by the Government of the League's plan of assistance, subject to certain reservations, details of which are contained in the letter . . . forwarded by first mail.'

"The plan has accordingly not been accepted as it stands, in its entirety and without reservations. We do not know the exact purpose of these reservations, since the announced letter has unfortunately not been received in time. But, according to the covering letter of the Liberian representative at Geneva, it would appear, even now, that they are more or less on the same lines as those put forward on several previous occasions and held to be unacceptable by the committee or by the Council."

The Rapporteur then stated that "The Council would doubtless regret being obliged to conclude from the communication of the Liberian Government that this Government refuses the plan of assistance . . ." In conclusion, he added: "My colleagues will doubtless agree with me that, if the above contingency should be realized, there would remain but to take note of the decision of Liberia, which would involve the cessation of the Council's activities in this matter.

"If, however, the announced letter or any other step taken by the Liberian Government should raise any new points for consideration, the Council might consider the question at its May session, in the course of which, in your Rapporteur's view, this question should be finally settled."

Notwithstanding this emphatic statement of the position assumed by the League a new declaration of constitutional objections was filed in March by C. L. Simpson, Secretary of State for Liberia. The main outline reiterated the previous exceptions. In response Joseph A. Avenol, Secretary-General of the League, said that its offer of service would be finally withdrawn if Liberia did not reverse its stand.

The Secretary-General declared that delay must end: "It will be remembered that on January 19 last the Council, in adopting the conclusions of the report submitted by the Polish representative, declared that should the plan not be accepted in its entirety and without reservation by its May session, the question should be considered as finally settled."

Chapter XII
LIBERIA AND THE FUTURE

DESPITE the combined efforts of so many world
forces, international willingness to help Liberia
still failed of realization. The situation plainly
drew to a crisis with the approach of Spring,
1934. With the May session of the League Council only a few weeks away it was hoped by all
parties at interest that the differences between
Liberia and the League still could be arranged.
But as the days passed even the most hopeful
observers failed to discern progress toward a
settlement.

Matters drifted until the 25th of April, when
the subject again was introduced in the House
of Lords for discussion. "... My excuse for doing
so is that your Lordships' House has never hesi-
tated to express the strongest disapproval of
gross misrule in whatever part of the world it has
occurred, and still less when that misrule has had
the result of causing unnecessary suffering and

misery to friendless and helpless people," said
Lord Meston. "Now that is the position in the
Republic of Liberia today. It has been exposed
that there is misrule, and that the indigenous
races are enduring a great deal of perfectly unnecessary misery and almost deliberate in-
justice."

By way of conclusion Lord Meston used
plainer language regarding Liberia than almost
any other speaker in the course of international
discussion up to that time:

". . . What I venture to suggest that your
Lordships would like to know is how far the
British Government are going to throw their
great influence into the scale, to induce the
Council of the League to take proper and adequate steps toward the restoration of good
government and ordinary humanity in this
derelict state."

Lord Lugard continued the discussion and
stressed the long delay which had taken place
without result, as far as a solution was concerned.
He devoted particular attention to the responsibility of the League, not only upon social and
humanitarian grounds, but especially by reason
of the League's obligations, contracted in its
own name by its own agents. Lord Lugard referred to conditions among the tribes, which
had prompted the League to send out Dr. Mackenzie as a mediator.

". . . He arrived in July, 1932, and found that

several Kru tribes had risen against the Government," said Lord Lugard, "but inter-tribal quarrels involving eighteen or twenty tribes had broken out, and he reports that 'four tribes comprising some 12,000 men, women and children had been driven into the bush and were in a state of advanced starvation.' The whole Kru coast had become engaged in inter-tribal fighting, which Dr. Mackenzie states had been instigated and supported by the Liberian politicians, and that the unrest had spread to the large settlements of Kru-men in the British Colonies of Sierra Leone and the Gold Coast, who were trying to smuggle arms and ammunition to their fellow tribesmen and were themselves anxious to join them. In the space of two months Dr. Mackenzie achieved the almost incredible feat of inducing these warring tribes to agree to keep the peace for the space of a year—namely, till August, 1933. Recognizing the temptation to fight so long as they retained their weapons, he reports that they surrendered them of their own accord, and 500 rifles and guns were handed over to the Liberian Government, which Dr. Mackenzie as an official of the League was bound to recognize as the *de facto* Government. His action received the full approval of the League Council."

Lord Lugard said it appeared that the Liberian Government, having got the upper hand, next began systematic abuse of the tribes. ". . . The latest information is," he continued, "that the

Chiefs arrested by the Negro Colonel Davis (of
the Frontier Force) are still in prison and some
are said to have died; that access to the sea on
which this seafaring and fishing tribe depend
has been closed; that President Barclay is on his
way to the interior, and troops sent in advance to
prepare for him have fired on villages and com-
mitted various outrages. . . . The tribes appeal to
the League for help now that their arms have
been surrendered in reliance upon the intervention of the League. The Chief who sends this
appeal says that he is in a dilemma. The President will summon him on arrival. If he refuses
to come, it will be regarded as a reason for attack.
If he obeys he has reason to fear that he will be
arrested as the other Chiefs were, and perhaps
share the fate of the seventy-five Chiefs—I am
told the right number was eighty-four—who
were executed in 1917."

Turning to another aspect of the Liberian
problem Lord Lugard said: ". . . The Negro
community in the United States appears to be
misinformed regarding the true state of affairs in
Liberia. We can understand and even sympathize
with their desire to prove to the world that the
Negro race is capable not only of self-government
but of governing a subject people; but the fact
that Professor Johnson, an American Negro, was
one of the Christy Commission which exposed
the slave-dealing and misrule, should show them
that so far from establishing the prestige of the

Negro race in the eyes of the world by champion-
ing the cause of the Liberian oligarchy, they are
seriously injuring it. Their assistance in carrying
out the League plan would be welcomed."

The speaker affirmed that in view of the multi-
plying evidence the American Government "...
cannot evade the responsibility of her long connection with and support of the Liberian Government in the past, or the share which men claiming American nationality have had, and I believe
still have, in the conduct of Liberian affairs. It
would seem that she (the United States) is in
the best position to issue that ultimatum which
would at once produce acceptance of the reforms which this costly discussion for five years
has failed to secure. All are agreed that nothing
short of the fear that worse may befall will induce the Liberian Government to agree, and as
His Majesty's Government very truly declared
three years ago, they are themselves incapable of
putting it into execution.

"... I venture with diffidence to make the suggestion that His Majesty's Government should
in the first place, jointly if possible with France,
invite the Council of the League to declare that
failing the acceptance without reserve of the
League's plan, any steps which the United States
Government may consider necessary to put an
end to present conditions would be welcomed;
and in the second place to exert British influence,
jointly with France, in pressing the American

Government to take the initiative in compelling
the Liberian Government to accept the scheme
of reform which has been prepared sympatheti-
cally and disinterestedly by the League Commission; or failing acceptance to put it into execution
herself (the United States) so far as the interior
is concerned, leaving the Government of Monrovia to enjoy autonomy in the coast enclave
which they actually occupy, and so avoid blood-
shed which may have repercussions beyond
Liberia."

Much the same view was set forth by Lord
Snell. ". . . I feel it right . . . that pressure might
be brought to bear upon Liberia by European
Governments to accept the League's plan," he
said. "If Liberia persistently and deliberately
refuses to accept that plan then her position as a
member of the League should be very seriously
questioned, with the understanding that, if she
were excluded from membership of the League,
the territory would become suitable for rule by a
mandatory power.

"I feel that the United States Government has
a great responsibility; but there is also this, that
an appeal to the Negro peoples of the world
might be made. This matter very closely touches
their honor, as the noble Lord has suggested. . . ."

The Lord Archbishop of Canterbury was the
next to rise. ". . . For many reasons and in many
ways I have such a solicitude for the peoples of
West Africa that I cannot on this occasion be

altogether silent," he observed. ". . . Surely it is one of the most lamentable tragedies of history that those who went forth 100 years ago as the liberators of the members of their own race, bearing the motto, 'Love of liberty has brought us here,' should be continuing there in the face of the civilized world as the oppressors of these people—about 10,000 Americo-Liberians tyrannizing over 2,000,000 members of inoffensive native tribes. . . . We cannot rest still while this blot upon the whole of the civilized world remains, and it would be a relief if we could know that His Majesty's Government, possibly in close coöperation with the United States of America, will do all that is possible to terminate a state of things which has become intolerable."

Viscount Cecil, a man with special knowledge of the Liberian situation, then said, referring to the plan of assistance: "I venture to assert to your Lordships that if any criticism could be made of it, it certainly is not that it disregarded the liberties of Liberia too much, but that, if anything, it did not go far enough to make really certain the good government of that country. I am sure that anything less than that would have been futile and dangerous. I agree most fully with what has been said by noble Lords who have preceded me that, in effect, the reservations suggested by Liberia amount to a total rejection of the plan. They really cut at the very root of it, because they propose that the Chief Adviser and

the other administrators should be entirely
under the control of the Liberian Government,
and should have no kind of jurisdiction except
that of tendering advice to the Liberian Government. I am sure that any plan of that kind would
be utterly futile, and the League would be most
ill-advised in my judgment if it consented to be
responsible in any way for a new reform on lines
of that kind.

"I think the present situation is this. Unless at
the last minute Liberia alters her attitude the
Council will be bound to declare at the next
meeting that the plan of assistance has failed,
and that as far as the request for assistance presented by the Liberian Government is concerned
it cannot be granted, because Liberia has declined
to carry out the only conditions on which it
would be safe, or decent or proper for the League
to assist her. . . ."

Lord Buxton declared that he thought the
evidence proved ". . . Liberia has in every possible way shown her unfitness to be a member of
the League, and that she certainly ought to be
'struck off the rolls.' But the question is, what
can be done after that? The difficulty appears to
most of us to lie in giving a proper answer and a
conclusive answer, or even any answer at all, to
the question: What will happen if that position
arises? I do not know whether it is fair to ask
the Government to make some suggestion in
regard to that matter; but after all they, with

France and America, will be responsible for the future of Liberia.

"I think it is clear that in the circumstances indicated Liberia ought to be struck off the League. She then becomes an independent country entirely apart from the League. The League ceases to have any jurisdiction over her; and who is then to undertake her protection and her suzerainty? Really the only country which is in a position to undertake that is the United States. She was responsible for Liberia's creation, and from the very inception of Liberia she has been responsible, both politically and financially, for her existence. I do not know, of course, what may be the views of the American Government, but I understand that they take a very serious view of the position; that they are very anxious to coöperate with England and France and other countries concerned, and that if they were pressed and if it were understood that they would have a free hand, they would be prepared to undertake the protectorate of Liberia. So far as I can judge the United States appears to be the only nation who can undertake it."

Liberian difficulties now had reached an advanced state where even a slight incident could embarrass the Republic. Such an incident arose when a Monrovian policeman entered the French Consulate to arrest a native employe. But the Consul, Eugene Emanuelli, defended his servant, protesting that the policeman was upon foreign soil. In an exchange of words the policeman struck the Consul, who forthwith demanded an apology from Liberia and cabled his Government for protection. After some delay Liberia apologized and punished the policeman.

The incident was not to end gracefully. A few days later, the 22nd of April, the French gunboat *Rigault de Genouilly* put into the harbor, and the Captain came ashore. He called upon the Liberian Secretary of State, accompanied by the Consul, and demanded a further apology. Secretary of State Simpson endeavored to justify the Liberian position, when the French Captain dramatically laid his sword upon the Secretary's desk and threatened to remain in port until he received a second apology. The Secretary being compelled to accede, the gunboat sailed away to the relief of everybody in Monrovia.

The whole world might be said to have had an inquiring eye turned toward Liberia, when leading citizens of that country caught the alarm. The 8th day of May, 1934, two of its former Presidents, two former Justices of the Supreme Court and other influential citizens submitted the following petition to President Barclay:

"We, the undersigned citizens of the Republic of Liberia in Montserrado County, exercising our constitutional rights to petition the Government on any cause affecting the interests of the state, hereby submit for your consideration and action the following:

"We recall that as the immediate outcome of the report of the International Commission of Enquiry, Your Excellency's Government found it necessary to apply to the League of Nations for assistance looking forward to the establishment of these reforms mentioned in said commission's report. This application resulted in the formulation by the League and the United States Government of a plan of assistance which was submitted to your Government for its acceptance.

"We further recall that at the last session of the Legislature said plan of assistance was accepted by them with such reservations which your Government considered necessary for the security of the state and the preservation of its autonomy. But these 'reservations,' we are informed, are considered by the League and the United States Government as tantamount to a rejection of the plan and they have intimated in definite language that unless the plan in its entirety is accepted by the Liberian Government at the ensuing session of the League Council convening on the 15th inst., the continued independent existence of our country is not guaranteed.

"In view of the conditions as outlined in the preceding paragraph the citizens feel a sense of insecurity and fear that grave consequences may ultimately result from any continued persistency on the part of the Government in its present attitude. This feeling of insecurity is intensified by recent press releases showing the attitude of Great Britain and the League toward Liberia, as well as by the admonition of the United States Government to our State Department to the effect that our acceptance of the League plan of assistance is our only guarantee of a continued independent existence. The United States Government, on whom we have always relied for aid and assistance in all of our national crises, recently also made it plain to our Liberian Secretary of State and to other responsible citizens that unless the plan of assistance is accepted in its entirety it would be under the painful necessity of refusing to intervene or offer any assistance in the event of possible aggression on our territory by any unfriendly nation.

"In consequence of the foregoing facts and seeing that the plan of assistance guarantees our autonomy, there would seem to be no alternative except for Your Excellency's Government to immediately withdraw its 'reservations' to the existing plan in its entirety and request the appointment of an American Chief Adviser to supervise its execution, who would report to the League as provided for in said plan. This in order to avert probable national disaster. And we, the citizens, therefore most respectfully urge, petition and enjoin upon you for the sake of the preservation of our beloved country, to see the wisdom of adopting such a course by or before

A Scene on the Miles of Good Roads Through Firestone Plantations (above)

Along the Road from Monrovia to Careysburg (below)

A Liberian Solomon with His Wives and Drummer Boy; Polygamy Is Common in the Hinterland

the 10th inst." A similar petition was filed by head men of the tribes.

This "10th instant" arrived, but without any change of attitude by the Liberian Government and the case reached the Council in about the form that it had been left months before. In this latest and greatest crisis of the Negro Republic, the views of Great Britain were expressed by Anthony Eden, British delegate, and were reported in the official minutes of the Council of the League meeting of May 18, 1934, as follows:

"The Council would recall that, under Article 23 (b) of the League Covenant, the members of the League undertook to secure just treatment of the native inhabitants of the territories under their control. It was the view of the United Kingdom Government—and he (Eden) stated it with the utmost earnestness—that Liberia had so grossly failed to observe this obligation attaching to her as a member of the League of Nations that the League would be quite entitled to consider her expulsion under Paragraph 4 of Article 16.

"His Majesty's Government fully realized that the expulsion of Liberia would not in itself be a step which would assist toward a solution of the Liberian problem. It was not, however, prepared, on general humanitarian grounds, to leave this matter, involving as it did questions of gross maladministration, in abeyance; and it proposed —provided that the Council concurred in its

view and that of the Rapporteur that the
League's offer of assistance to Liberia must now
be withdrawn—to approach the United States
Government on the subject since that Government appeared to the United Kingdom Government to be the one most closely associated, both
historically and economically, with Liberia. His
Majesty's Government would make that approach in a desire to coöperate with the United
States Government in an attempt to find a
remedy for a state of affairs the real tragedy of
which, in its unrelieved record of misery and misgovernment, must be apparent to every informed
and unprejudiced observer." The Council then
formally withdrew its offer of assistance, but
did not expel the accused member.

Although the Liberian incident has passed
from the slate of the League, at least for the
time being, it continues to occupy a leading
place in the thoughts of European ministers. Sir
John Simon, the British Secretary for Foreign
Affairs, addressed a note the 29th of May to
Sir Ronald Lindsay, British Ambassador in
Washington, with the request that he transmit
its sense to the American Government. This
note* reviewed at length the progress of Liberian
affairs, concluding with two paragraphs which
forcibly presented the British view:

"5. To sum up. Greatly to the regret of His
Majesty's Government, the League's attempt to

*See Appendix B, page 208.

assist Liberia has not been successful. Liberia rejected, on the financial side, the not ungenerous terms obtained for her by the League from her chief foreign creditor, the Finance Corporation of America. Indeed, she has, I understand, repudiated most of her obligations to that body. On the administrative side she made reservations which, if accepted, would render it impossible for the white officials, who were to be appointed under the League plan, to secure any serious administrative reform. In these circumstances the League Council have felt impelled to withdraw the plan of assistance offered to Liberia, and His Majesty's Government feel that the whole situation must be reconsidered. They feel that it would be a dereliction of duty to civilization if the misgovernment of the native tribes by Liberia were to be allowed to continue, resulting, as it would infallibly result, in the encouragement of such evils as slave trading and the slaughter and maltreatment of 2,000,000 natives by the corrupt and inefficient oligarchy of Monrovia. At the same time His Majesty's government cannot believe that the pressure of public opinion, or even the threat of exclusion of Liberia from the League, if that should be practicable, will be adequate to create any real and lasting improvement in Liberia. They are aware of the deep interest which the United States Government have always taken in the fortunes of this state, which, indeed, owes its foundation to American enterprise and philanthropy. On the material side, Liberia is rendered dependent upon the United States Government by the extent to which her financial machinery is already in American hands and organized in conformity with a contract entered into between the Liberian Government and an American corporation. His Majesty's Government cannot, therefore, doubt that the United States Government have been as much perturbed as have they themselves by the course of recent events, and they would be grateful for an indication of the policy which the United States Government would in the circumstances recommend. For their own part, His Majesty's Government are ready to coöperate to the utmost of their power in any well-considered measures which the United States Government may consider appropriate to the occasion.

"6. The enclosed copy of the minutes of the recently concluded session of the League Council will serve to complete for Your Excellency the picture of the present situation, of which the United States Government, who were again represented at Geneva by Mr. Reber, will no doubt be fully informed. I shall be glad if you will address to the United States Government a note on the lines of the preceding paragraphs."

While these events were under way in Europe, 12,000,000 Negroes of the United States were aroused to the threatened extinction of the Liberian Republic and have joined in a concerted effort to preserve the nation which has such intimate ties with the Negroes of the United States. An outgrowth of this movement is an attempt to establish a strictly American plan of assistance for Liberia.

At a conference of Negro religious leaders held in Washington February 7 under the auspices of the Negro Foreign Mission Boards active in Liberia, resolutions were adopted and later presented to Secretary of State Hull by a committee. They read in part:

"1. That the Government of the United States be urged to resume diplomatic relations with the Republic of Liberia.

"2. That the League of Nations plan of assistance to Liberia in her present crisis be thoroughly considered in the light and spirit of Liberia's reservations, and that the Liberian Government be urged to do everything possible to retain the traditional interest and support of the American Government.

"a. (The 'reservations' here referred to are those that may not have been considered by the League of Nations.)

"b. (It was the general feeling of the conference that the acceptance of the plan as it may finally be approved by the League of Nations after consideration of reservations adopted by the Liberian Legislature January 12, 1934, is essential to the political independence and stability of Liberia and its economic and social progress.)

"c. (Further, it was the feeling of the conference that the appointment of an American Adviser will greatly contribute to the restoration of the traditional interest and support of the American people who have been Liberia's main dependence during all the years of her history.)

"3. That in view of the large interests in Liberia of men and money invested by the respective foreign boards, channels of communication be kept open so that the missionary effort remain under the guidance of American influence.

"Finally, it is recommended that representatives of the respective boards seek to convey to Negro public opinion in America and to all right-thinking Americans and to the Liberian Government an earnest desire to help preserve the sovereignty and autonomy of Liberia. It is our earnest desire that there be resumed the historical relationship of confidence between the U. S. Department of State and the Government of Liberia. Liberia was founded as a colony for freed American Negroes by the American Colonization Society in 1822. Our Government, therefore, has a duty and responsibility which cannot be evaded. Liberia also has a duty and responsibility to maintain a stable government which will command the respect of the powers of the world."

Numerous other representative bodies of Negroes have urged upon official quarters the need for an American plan of assistance. President

Roosevelt recently received the following message from Dr. Mary Fitzbutler Waring, president of The National Association of Colored Women:

"The Negro Women of America are intensely interested in future of Liberian Republic. Representing The National Association of Colored Women, comprising more than 50,000 members, we earnestly appeal to you to aid our sister Republic, bound to us by historic ties, by initiating for Liberia an American plan of assistance."

A number of messages to the same purpose have reached the White House and Department of State, and representations also were made direct to Monrovia by L. K. Williams, President of the National Baptist Convention, which embraces 3,000,000 members. In a cable message to President Barclay he said: "American Negroes intensely concerned in Liberia's future respectfully urge you to ask American Government to provide plan of assistance."

Religious, fraternal, civic and business groups of the race daily express themselves regarding Liberia.

A resolution was passed by Bishops of the African Methodist Episcopal Church at the annual meeting of the Foreign and Home Mission Board, held in New York June 22:

"Whereas, the Republic of Liberia is in serious danger of being mandated by some European Power, and

"Whereas, the preservation of Liberia's political independence and the rehabilitation of her economic and social structures are of deep concern to the American Negro, and

"Whereas, the plan of assistance formulated by the League of Nations has been rejected by the Republic of Liberia,

"Be it resolved, that the Home and Foreign Mission Board of the African Methodist Episcopal Church, whose membership is composed of Bishops and other officers of the denomination, appeal to the President of the United States and respectfully importune that the American Government undertake the responsibility of establishing needed reforms in the Republic of Liberia by providing a plan of assistance supervised by Americans, which would insure the country of its continued sovereignty and autonomy, guarantee the administration of law and order and furnish Liberia with some financial program, thereby enabling her to win the confidence of the nations of the world and permit her to exert an influence for good in international affairs."

Such is the account of an historic international effort to assist Liberia; an effort that finally failed. What the nation's fate will be in the future no one can foresee. With the powers of Europe demanding corrective action upon their own account and through the League of Nations; a demand supported by the majority of Liberian citizens and the natives of that country as well;

and a demand further supplemented by the Negroes and many representative organizations of the United States, it would seem that the American Government is now confronted with the necessity of assisting Liberia to adjust her difficulties and so maintain the century-old policy of protecting our African ward, even against its own deeds.

LIBERIA

DOCUMENTS RELATING TO THE PLAN OF ASSISTANCE PROPOSED BY THE LEAGUE OF NATIONS

(Reprinted from the Official Record of the United States Department of State, November 19, 1933)

APPENDIX A

ENDORSEMENT OF THE PLAN BY THE DEPART-
MENT OF STATE, NOVEMBER 19, 1933

In connection with the request by Liberia for the assistance
of the League of Nations, and the Plan of Assistance which was
adopted by the Council Committee on Liberia on October 13,
1933, and endorsed by the Council on the following day, the
Department is herewith issuing certain documents, which have
already been made public in Geneva.

The American Government considers that the Plan is fair
and practical, that it contains ample safeguards for Liberia, and
that it will lead to a solution of Liberia's problems.

It will be recalled that the Liberian request for the assistance of the League has been under consideration for nearly
three years by the League Committee, in whose work the American Government has participated. Every phase of the situation
has been examined by impartial experts, whose work was
passed upon by the Committee representing eight separate governments in addition to Liberia, and finally by the Council of
the League. Prolonged and sympathetic consideration has been
given by the Committee to all the Liberian views, including a
rehearing on the entire matter in October 1933 at the request
of the Liberian Government.

A full discussion of these matters since the establishment of
the League Committee on Liberia in January 1931 appears in
the Report of the Committee to the Council.

The American Government expects Liberia to accept the
Plan of Assistance and will be pleased in this case to coöperate
in its successful execution. Should the present administration at
Monrovia reject this opportunity, such action could only be construed as opposition to reforms the urgent desirability of which
has been apparent for over three years, and as indifference to
the welfare of the million and a half native people of Liberia.

LEAGUE OF NATIONS

C.595.M.277.1933.VII.
GENEVA, *October 14th, 1933.*

COMMITTEE OF THE COUNCIL APPOINTED TO EXAMINE THE PROBLEM RAISED BY THE LIBERIAN GOVERNMENT'S REQUEST FOR ASSISTANCE.

FINAL REPORT OF THE COMMITTEE TO THE COUNCIL.
ADOPTED ON OCTOBER 13TH, 1933.

1. In January 1931 the Liberian Government informed[1] the Council that it had decided to adopt in principle the recommendations of the International Commission of Enquiry[2] to the full extent of its resources. It pointed out that it intended to take further steps as soon as the state of its finances permitted and expressed the desire for the general and specific financial and health assistance of the League of Nations with a view to giving effect to the said recommendations.[3]

The Council examined the Liberian request for assistance at its meeting of January 24th, 1931, and appointed a Committtee to consider the means whereby it would be possible to assist the Liberian Government.

The American Government was invited to participate in the work of the Committee and accepted.

The Committee has kept the Council thoroughly conversant with the progress of its work. It may be recalled that three experts on administration, finance and public health visited Liberia in June and July 1931 on behalf of the Committee.

Their report and the information made available to the experts by the Liberian Government formed the basis on which the Committee drew up the "General Principles of the Plan of Assistance," which were adopted on September 27th, 1932, by the Committee and accepted by the Liberian Government.[4]

[1] C.50.M.27.1931.VI.

[2] C.658.M.272.1930.VI.

[3] C.134.1931.VI.

[4] C.720.1932.VII. [The text of the General Principles was printed in *Press Releases,* Weekly Issue No. 159, Saturday, Oct. 15, 1932, pp. 240–244.—EDITOR.]

The acceptance by the Liberian Government was however conditional on a satisfactory outcome of the negotiations to be undertaken between the Government of Liberia on the one hand and the Finance Corporation of America on the other. It was further arranged with the approval of the Liberian Government that in these negotiations they might have the assistance of Mr. Ligthart and the Financial Organisation of the League.

The financial negotiations took place in London in June 1933 and resulted in a report presented by Mr. Th. Ligthart, the Financial Expert to the Committee.

On the basis of the General Principles and Mr. Ligthart's report, the Committee drew up a Protocol[5] to be accepted by the Council and to be signed by the Liberian Government.

The Liberian Government have made certain observations[6] in connection with the Protocol. The Committee has considered most carefully the points raised by the Liberian Government.

Amongst the principal points raised by the Liberian delegation were the constitutional aspects of the Plan. These were carefully examined and the Committee was of opinion that the foreign advisers should have sufficient power to ensure the satisfactory functioning of the Plan. The methods by which these powers should be granted by the Liberian Government to the foreign administrators was a question for decision by the Liberian Government itself. The Committee is of opinion that the present Plan is in close accord with the request for assistance put forward by the Government of Liberia in the letter of the Permanent Delegate of January 23rd, 1931, to the Council[7] and if accepted by the Liberian Government will ensure the political independence of the Republic and avoid infringement of its territorial integrity and the exercise of its sovereign rights.

The Plan provides for the appointment by the Council of the League of Nations of a Chief Adviser, three Provincial Commissioners, three Deputy Provincial Commissioners and two medical officers.

The Chief Adviser will exercise a general supervision over the execution of the Plan and coördinate the work of the for-

[5] C.421.M.214.1933.VII.
[6] C.Liberia./42.
[7] C.134.1931.VI.

eign experts functioning as advisers to the Liberian Government. The Liberian Government undertakes to follow the advice of the Chief Adviser. Provision has also been made that in cases of disagreement a final decision shall be taken by the Council.

Inasmuch as the Chief Adviser supervises the execution of the Plan of Assistance and serves to coördinate the work of all the foreign experts, it is clearly necessary that provision must be made for the latter closely to collaborate with the Chief Adviser. It was for this reason that the Committee was unable to accept the suggestion of the Liberian representative that the activities of the Chief Adviser should be confined to giving advice to the Central Government and that the foreign experts provided for in the Plan should be responsible only to the Central Government.

On the other hand, the Committee was of opinion that the foreign experts appointed under the Plan should be attached to the corresponding Department of the Central Government and should work in close association with the Head of the corresponding Department. While it was necessary for the Committee to define to some extent the relative position and powers of the various foreign administrators, it is clear that the full confidence of the Liberian Government and its close coöperation with the foreign specialists are essential for the satisfactory functioning of any Plan of Assistance.

The Committee discussed the possibility of defining in the Protocol the sphere within which the Chief Adviser should be empowered to give advice which must be followed by the Government of Liberia, but was obliged to recognise the impracticability of attempting a formal definition of his powers. The Committee assured the Liberian Government that it was amply protected against any undesirable infringements of its powers by two facts. In the first place any official appointed as Chief Adviser by the Council would be selected with the greatest care and would be a man of tact and understanding who would only exercise his powers in the spirit of the Plan of Assistance. In the second place, the Liberian Government was further protected by its right to appeal to the Council of the League of Nations under whose auspices the Plan of Assistance was drawn up.

It was agreed that the Chief Adviser ought not be of the same nationality of the Financial Adviser nor should he be of the nationality of any country which had territory adjacent to Liberia.[8]

The Liberian representative pointed out that in the existing division of the country into three provinces the Legislature had excluded from the provinces the incorporated towns. The Committee felt it was essential that for the purpose of the Plan the whole territory of the Republic should be included in the three Provinces as had been agreed to previously by the Liberian Government.

It will be remembered that the Liberian Government accepted last year the appointment of three foreign Provincial Commissioners and three foreign Deputy Provincial Commissioners. The Liberian delegation asked that the three Deputy Commissioners should be Liberians. The Committee felt that the question of the three Deputies being Liberians must be left to the judgment of the Chief Adviser.

With regard to the messengers to be attached to each Provincial Commissioner, the question as to whether or not these should be armed was fully discussed at the meeting last year. It was then decided and agreed to by the Liberian Government that this question should be left for decision by the Chief Adviser. In response to the Liberian delegation's representations, the Committee has now decided that the question as to whether the messengers should be armed or not shall be left for decision by the Liberian Government upon the recommendation of the Chief Adviser.

With regard to the use of troops in the various Provinces, the Liberian representative urged that no body of troops should be placed under the command of foreigners. The Committee felt that it would be inadvisable to limit the choice of commanders in the text of the plan. The question of the command of the frontier force was therefore left for discussion between the Liberian Government and the Chief Adviser during the currency of the plan.

With regard to finance, the Committee in the first place would draw attention to the fact that at the present time the

[8]See statement made by the American delegate on this subject (Annex I).

whole of the financial administration is to a great extent dependent upon the Loan Agreement. The Committee was therefore of the opinion that there could be no effective plan outlined unless this included provisions for the financial administration, especially in view of the fact that during the time that the Plan is in force certain administrative provisions of the Loan Agreement cease to be effective. It was for this reason that Articles 6, 7, 8, 9, 10 and 11 of Chapter 3 were included in the Committee's plan, and the Committee was therefore unable to accept the Liberian Government's amendment that these be deleted. These articles are substantially the same as the corresponding articles in the Loan Agreement, except in the case of Articles 8 and 9. The difference in these articles made by the Committee with the consent of the Finance Corporation only serve to bring the control of both the assigned and unassigned revenue under the advice of the Financial Adviser and the Chief Adviser.

The question as to whether the sum of 300,000 Liberian dollars as fixed by the Committee's Financial Expert, was sufficient, was raised by the Liberian delegation, which suggested the figure of 375,000 Liberian dollars. The Financial Expert pointed out to the Committee that this figure was only one suggested tentatively by him by way of example and was for the first year of the Plan only. It was clear that in view of the changing currencies and the varying economic conditions it was impossible to fix a budget here and now. Budgets would have to be fixed by the Liberian Government in consultation with the Chief Adviser and the Financial Adviser.

The Financial Expert also pointed out to the Committee that the sum of 300,000 Liberian dollars was global and constituted in his opinion the proportion of the revenue of Liberia which could be fairly expended in running expenses in view of Liberia's present obligations. The question of the detailed allocation of the 300,000 Liberian dollars and the rest of the budget would, of course, be left for decision between the Liberian Government, the Chief Adviser and the Financial Adviser.

With regard to the salaries of Liberian officials, the Financial Expert pointed out the urgent necessity for financial sacrifices in the present state of Liberia, and further emphasised that under the Plan salaries provided for would be paid in full, which had not always been the case.

The Liberian delegation raised the question of the provision of money for education. The Committee strongly emphasised the necessity for expenditure in this direction, but felt the whole question was one to be decided by the Liberian Government in consultation with the Chief Adviser and the Financial Adviser at the time the budget was prepared.

The Committee then proceeded to discuss the Liberian objection that the total cost of the Plan was excessive and in particular the salaries of the foreign administrators were too generous. The Financial Expert pointed out in this connection that the salaries to be paid to the foreign administrators were to a great extent already fixed, inasmuch as it was agreed to pay these on the scale of those obtaining for officials of similar rank serving in West Africa. He further urged that the sum of 54,000 Liberian dollars for road construction was not excessive.

The Liberian delegation's attention was also drawn to the fact that in the original Plan of the experts the sum provided for the Plan was 400,000 dollars, and it had already been very considerably reduced to the figure of 150,000 dollars.

The Financial Expert reminded the Committee that he had based his figures on the exchange values obtaining in June 1933, and that should violent fluctuations occur in either the United States dollar or the Liberian dollar, the figures given in the report would call for revision. This revision would be effected by the Liberian Government in agreement with the Chief Adviser and the Financial Adviser.

The Committee proceeded to consider the Liberian Government's objection to a further increase in their financial obligations to the Finance Corporation. The Financial Expert pointed out in the first place that two factors were essential. Firstly it was necessary to obtain an initial working capital fund in order to put the plan into operation, and secondly it was essential to have a guarantee covering the salaries and incidental expenses of the contract, which would be made with the various foreign administrators. It was clear that if it were possible to meet these sums out of current revenue this would be done. But if not, an initial working capital fund must be immediately established and for this purpose must be borrowed if the Plan were to come into operation.

The Financial Expert stressed the fact that the proposed loan of 150,000 U. S. dollars would only occur during the first year as the sum would be made up annually from current revenues.

The Financial Expert reminded the Committee that one of the fundamental results of the establishment of the Plan would be the renewal of prosperity with resulting increased revenue. He did not anticipate that in actual practice it would be necessary to call upon the guarantees at all during the five years, but it was essential for the guarantee to exist; whether it was taken up or not depended to a great extent upon the economies effected by the Liberian Government.

In this connection the Financial Expert outlined the concessions that had been given by the Financial Corporation during the negotiations in London in 1933. These included:

a) Priority to the running costs of the Liberian Government over the payment of interest and the salaries of the financial advisers;

b) Priority to the cost of the Plan of Assistance over the payment of interest on the Loan;

c) Renunciation of interest accruing during any one year if the total revenue of the Liberian Government is insufficient to meet the first two priorities. This amounts, in fact, to a moratorium throughout the five years unless the Liberian Government's revenue amounts to over Lib. $500,000 or more if it was decided that Lib. $300,000 was insufficient for the operating expenses of the Government or that the figures of the Plan of Assistance had to be revised in view of currency fluctuation.

d) Permanent reduction of the rate of interest from 7% to 5%. This and other permanent savings effected through reduction in the salaries of fiscal staff, et cetera, will result in a present annual saving to Liberia of about U. S. $62,000.

e) Guarantee by the Finance Corporation of the salaries and leave expenses of the foreign advisers

during the period of five years when these expenses cannot be met out of current revenues.
f) Guarantee of an immediate loan of $150,000 as
initial working capital to start the Plan of Assistance.

In other words, there will be a permanent saving to the
Liberian Government of U.S. $62,000, on the basis of the bonds
at present outstanding, plus an arrangement whereby the
amount of U.S. $125,000, owed annually by the Liberian Gov-
ernment under the amended Loan Agreement, will be absolutely renounced by the Finance Corporation during the operation of the Plan if the total revenue of the Liberian Government is insufficient first to meet the operating expenses of the
Government, the cost of the Plan of Assistance, and the salaries
of Loan officials.

The Committee again discussed the question of arrears apart
from the Loan but decided to adhere to the recommendation
made by Mr. Ligthart in June last.[9]

In conclusion the Committee reminded the Liberian delegation that the request of the Government of Liberia was for the
assistance of the League of Nations. A Plan had now been
established which outlined the conditions under which the
League was prepared to grant assistance to Liberia. Whether
such assistance was accepted or not on the terms offered depended entirely on the desire of the Liberian Government. The
Committee pointed out that it had carefully considered and expressed an opinion on each of the amendments raised by the
Liberian delegation, and the present Plan represented the considered conditions upon which assistance could, in the opinion
of the Committee, only be granted to Liberia. The Committee
emphasised that its plan must be regarded as a whole, and that
the financial advantages contained in the plan are, of course,
conditional on the administrative part of the Plan.

During the course of the discussions in Committee, the Liberian representative made several reservations and when in
the course of this report the Committee is said to have arrived

[9] See Annex II.

at certain opinions due regard must be had to these reservations.

The draft Protocol adopted by the Committee is annexed.[10]

ANNEX I. STATEMENT MADE BY THE AMERICAN REPRESENTATIVE, OCTOBER 9TH, 1933.

The American Government has not heretofore expressed itself before the Committee on the question of the nationality of the Chief Adviser to Liberia under the proposed League Plan of Assistance. It has been the personal view of the American Representative that what was needed was a man of outstanding character, competence and ability, irrespective of his nationality, but that a Chief Adviser of American nationality might be especially desirable from the point of view of Liberia, in that his presence might promote an increase in contributions by various interested organisations in the United States for educational, religious and medical purposes.

The American Government is aware that there have been objections in certain quarters to an American Chief Adviser. It believes that it is of vital importance that a Plan of Assistance to Liberia should be established without delay. The American Government does not maintain that the Chief Adviser should be of American nationality.

ANNEX II. CONCERNING THE QUESTION OF ARREARS APART FROM THE LOAN.

The Liberian delegation informed the Committee that the Government had already provided for the payment of arrears by the issue of internal 3% bonds. With regard to this issue the American delegation questioned the legality of this procedure and made the following statement:

"The American Government contests the right of the Liberian Government to issue these internal bonds. Such action

[10]See Annex III.

would, if taken, constitute a direct violation of the Covenant of the Republic of Liberia as set forth specifically in Article XV of the Loan Agreement which was duly ratified by the Liberian Legislature and approved by the President and is therefore part of the Statutory Law. The Liberian 'law' of January 1933 to which the Liberian Representative has referred is unilateral and illegal. Furthermore, such action would be in direct opposition to the recommendations formulated in June 1933 and repeated to the Council Committee on Liberia by M. Ligthart, the Financial Expert of the Liberian Government's choice, in October 1933, to the effect that the floating debt should be retired from revenues without recourse to the issue of any internal bonds.

"With respect to the statement of the Liberian Representative that the issue of internal bonds had on one occasion been recommended by Mr. Ligthart, the American Representative submits, with the assent of Mr. Ligthart, that this recommendation was in fact a suggestion for the Liberian Government to raise in discussion with the Finance Corporation of America with a view to obtaining the agreement of the Corporation to this step. This agreement has not been obtained. Moreover, Mr. Ligthart's suggestion was made in 1931, at a time when the Liberian Government was not in default on the service of the Finance Corporation Loan."

The Financial Expert expressed his concurrence with the American observations.

ANNEX III. DRAFT PROTOCOL ESTABLISHING A PLAN OF ASSISTANCE FOR LIBERIA.

WHEREAS the Liberian Government has requested assistance from the League of Nations in the establishment of reforms in the administration and finances of the Republic of Liberia;

AND WHEREAS the Council of the League of Nations, after examination of the administration and financial situation of Liberia, in collaboration with representatives of the Government of Liberia, by a Committee appointed by the Council and a Committee of Experts, has agreed to the plan of assistance established by the present Protocol and the Annex thereto, which were approved by the Council by its resolution of 1933;

AND WHEREAS the plan is intended to ensure the political independence of the Republic of Liberia, and to avoid infringing in any way its territorial integrity or the exercise by its Government of its sovereign rights;

The undersigned, duly authorised, accepts on behalf of the Government of Liberia the following provisions:

Chapter I—ADMINISTRATION

ARTICLE 1.

1. For administrative purposes, the territory of the Republic of Liberia is already divided into three provinces by the legislative authority of Liberia.

2. It is understood that the whole territory of the Republic is to be included within the three provinces.

3. Unless otherwise fixed by the Liberian Government in agreement with the Chief Adviser, whose appointment is provided for in Chapter IV:

(a) The Western Province shall extend from the Anglo-Liberian boundary on the north-west to the St. Paul River, and from the Atlantic Ocean to the Franco-Liberian boundary;

(b) The Central Province shall extend from the St. Paul River to the Cestos or Nuon River, and from the Atlantic Ocean to the Franco-Liberian boundary; and

(c) The Eastern Province shall extend from the Cestos or Nuon River to the Cavalla River, and from the Atlantic Ocean to the Franco-Liberian boundary.

ARTICLE 2.

1. Each province shall be administered by a Provincial Commissioner assisted by a Deputy Commissioner.

2. The Provincial Commissioner is responsible to the Chief Adviser and, as representative of the executive power, to the President of the Republic of Liberia, through the intermediary

of the Secretary of the Interior, with the understanding that no instructions, regulations or orders shall be issued to the Provincial Commissioner except after consultation with and approval of the Chief Adviser.

3. It shall be his duty to see that the laws and regulations are carried out, and he shall be responsible for public peace and order.

ARTICLE 3.

1. To ensure public order, the Commissioners will have under their direct orders a corps of messengers, the numbers of which will be settled by the Liberian Government in consultation with the Chief Adviser.

The Government of Liberia shall decide, on the recommendation of the Chief Adviser, whether the messengers are to be armed or not.

2. Neither the "Frontier Force" nor any other military organisation of Liberia may intervene in the provinces, except at the request of the Provincial Commissioner, and then only within what the latter considers to be the necessities of the case.

ARTICLE 4.

1. The Government of Liberia will engage three foreign specialists as Commissioners of the three provinces, and three other persons as deputies of the said Commissioners. They shall be designated by the Council of the League of Nations and approved by the President of the Republic of Liberia and appointed by him.

2. Only the three Provincial Commissioners will be appointed immediately, in order to proceed to Liberia with the Chief Adviser. The Deputy Commissioners will be appointed later, as provided for in Chapter IV.

3. With the approval of the Chief Adviser, any or all of the three deputies may be Liberians. In such case, their appointment shall be made by the President of the Republic, on the proposal of the Chief Adviser.

4. The foreign specialists who act as Provincial Commissioners will undertake the administrative training of the Liberian officials by whom they will be succeeded on the expira-

tion of their contracts if the Chief Adviser considers the said Liberians to be able to perform their duties satisfactorily.

Chapter II—HEALTH.

ARTICLE 5.

1. The Liberian Government agrees in principle to engage two whole-time medical officers for hospital and health work. They shall carry out all the ordinarily accepted duties of a medical officer of health in a tropical country.

2. They will be designated by the Council of the League of Nations and approved by the President of the Republic of Liberia and appointed by him. One will be appointed immediately and the other as soon as the Chief Adviser thinks it opportune.

3. They will be responsible to the Chief Adviser and to the President of Liberia.

4. As regards the appointment of the second medical officer, the President of Liberia, in consultation with the Chief Adviser, will have regard to the financial resources available.

Chapter III—FINANCE

ARTICLE 6.

1. The Liberian Government shall continue to appoint to its service a Financial Adviser, together with a certain number of assistants, as provided for in the Loan Agreement of September 1st, 1926, and any contractual modification thereof by and between the Republic of Liberia, the Finance Corporation of America and the National City Bank of New York, made before this Protocol comes into force.

ARTICLE 7.

2. It shall be the duty of the Financial Adviser and his collaborators to ensure the efficient organisation and functioning of the Liberian fiscal services and also the regular payment of the service of the loan advanced by the Finance Corporation of America, and they shall have all the powers necessary for their purposes.

ARTICLE 8.

The Financial Adviser shall have the right of supervision over all questions within the financial sphere and shall have the right, more particularly, to make sure that the credits allocated are being judiciously applied for the purposes stipulated.

ARTICLE 9.

All revenues and receipts of the Liberian Government (including import and export duties of every description, poll-tax, and all other imposts, taxes and receipts of the Republic) shall be collected under the supervision and direction of the Financial Adviser and his collaborators, who shall coöperate with the officials responsible for collection and, as regards provincial revenues and receipts, with the Provincial Commissioners.

ARTICLE 10.

All revenues and receipts of the Government shall be deposited in a bank designated as the official depository in accordance with Article XVIII of the Loan Agreement of 1926, or any agreement supplementary thereto.

ARTICLE 11.

No commitment in respect of expenditure shall be entered into and no sum shall be withdrawn from the Government funds deposited in the bank without the approval of the Financial Adviser.

ARTICLE 12.

Any disagreement between the Liberian Government or any official thereof and the Financial Adviser shall be submitted to the Chief Adviser, who will arbitrate thereon and will make to the Council of the League of Nations a report which shall be communicated to the Government of the United States of America. This shall in no way modify or restrict the provision for arbitration between the Parties to the Loan Agreement of

1926, as provided in Article XXV of that Agreement, or any contractual modification thereof made before this Protocol comes into force.

Chapter IV.—Coördination of Measures of Reform and Liaison with the League of Nations.

Article 13.

1. A Chief Adviser shall be appointed by the Council of the League of Nations with the acceptance (agrément) of the President of the Republic of Liberia.[11] This adviser shall be responsible to and removable by the Council of the League of Nations. He shall be attached to the Central Government, in order to give it the benefit of his advice, to supervise the execution of the Plan of Assistance and to coördinate the work of the foreign experts.

2. The Chief Adviser shall proceed with the three Provincial Commissioners as soon as possible to Liberia and assume his activities. He will prepare, in collaboration with the President of the Republic of Liberia and with the assistance of the advisers provided in the preceding chapters, the progressive details of the Plan of Assistance upon the principles agreed to in this Protocol, and taking account of the draft plan drawn up by the experts and of the discussions that have taken place in the Committee referred to in the Preamble.

3. The Liberian Government undertakes to collaborate with the Chief Adviser, and, subject to the reservation hereafter provided in the following article, to act in accordance with his advice and recommendations, and grant him all facilities for the performance of his duties throughout his term of office. It hereby agrees to delegate to the Chief Adviser sufficient authority for the effective execution of the plan of assistance in accordance with his powers defined in the first two paragraphs of the present article. The Chief Adviser may, in particular, ask for any documents and official reports he may require, and may make such investigations as he may think fit in the country.

[11]It is understood that the Chief Adviser should not belong to the same nationality as the Financial Adviser or to the nationality of any country which has territory adjacent to Liberia.

ARTICLE 14.

1. The Liberian Government may, if it considers necessary, refer any question to the Council of the League of Nations, including any question upon which there is any disagreement between the Liberian Government and the Chief Adviser.

2. Should it consider that the recommendations made by the Chief Adviser are in violation of the existing constitution of the Republic, it may ask the Council to refer the question to the Permanent Court of International Justice for an advisory opinion.

3. Until a decision has been given by the Council, the Liberian Government undertakes to comply with the recommendations made by the Chief Adviser, provided that, on the application of the Liberian Government, the Council of the League of Nations, or the acting President thereof, may decide that the execution of these recommendations shall be suspended pending the final decision of the Council.

4. The Chief Adviser shall make such communications as he may think fit to the Council of the League of Nations, provided he shall report at least every quarter upon the progress of his work and the execution of the plan of reforms, and will file a copy of the report with the Government of Liberia, to be kept in the archives of the Republic.

5. Should the Council consider that the Liberian Government has disregarded the undertakings given in the present Protocol, it may declare that the present Protocol has lapsed and that consequently the arrangements entered into with the Finance Corporation of America for the execution of the plan of assistance are no longer binding on this company. In such case, compensation to be fixed by the Council shall be paid to the Chief Adviser and other specialists appointed or designated by the Council, and any balance of the working capital provided for in the report of Mr. Ligthart reproduced in the Annex shall be applied to immediate amortisation of bonds issued under the Loan Agreement of 1926 or any agreement supplementary thereto.

6. In urgent cases, the acting President of the Council may act on behalf of the Council, provided that he refers the matter to the Council as soon as possible.

ARTICLE 15.

1. The Chief Adviser shall receive a salary not exceeding U. S. $12,000.

2. If it is found possible to fix the Chief Adviser's salary at a figure lower than U. S. $12,000, this will be done.

Chapter V.—DURATION OF THE PLAN OF ASSISTANCE.

ARTICLE 16.

The plan of assistance will terminate and the present Protocol will cease to be in force after a period of five years from the date of nomination of the Chief Adviser by the Council of the League of Nations, unless the Liberian Government intimates its desire that it should continue. In the latter case, the Council of the League of Nations may reconsider whether it desires to continue its coöperation and under what conditions.

Chapter VI.—GENERAL PROVISIONS.

ARTICLE 17.

1. All the powers exercisable by the Council of the League of Nations under the provisions of the present Protocol, except under Chapter IV (Article 14, paragraph 5) and Chapter V, may, unless otherwise decided by the Council, be exercised, and final decisions may be taken, by a standing committee which will be appointed by the Council.

2. The powers given to the President-in-office of the Council can not be delegated to the President of the committee mentioned above.

ARTICLE 18.

1. For the purposes of Chapter IV, Article 14, paragraph 5, the Council of the League of Nations shall take all decisions by a unanimous vote, Liberia's vote not counting in the calculation of such unanimity.

2. Subject to the provisions of Article 18, paragraph 1, and with the exception of the action proposed under Chapter V, all decisions to be taken in virtue of the present Protocol by the Council or the committee appointed by the Council shall be taken by a two-thirds majority.

ARTICLE 19.

1. The salaries of the foreign specialists will be fixed by the Council of the League of Nations, on the basis of the salaries of the similar officials of neighbouring colonies.

2. Account will be taken of the special conditions which should be granted to officials of international status, and also, of course, of the financial resources available.

3. The foreign experts appointed under the Plan shall be attached to the relevant department concerned and shall work in association with the head of that department.

ARTICLE 20.

The foreign specialists mentioned in Chapters I and II may be replaced for adequate reasons with the consent of the Council of the League of Nations.

ARTICLE 21.

Liberia accepts and undertakes, so far as it is concerned, to give effect to the report of Mr. Ligthart, as reproduced in the Annex to the present Protocol.

ARTICLE 22.

The Liberian Government undertakes forthwith, after the signature of the present Protocol, to lay before the Liberian Legislature a draft law, or to take such other measures as are necessary, to give during the operation of the Plan of Assistance to any Government which may be in power the necessary authority to take all measures which may be necessary to enable full force and effect to be given to all the provisions of the present Protocol and its annexes.

ARTICLE 23.

In the event of any discrepancy between the English and French texts of the present Protocol or the Annex, the English text shall prevail.

ARTICLE 24.

1. The present Protocol shall be ratified by Liberia and the instrument of ratification shall be deposited with the Secretariat of the League of Nations.

2. The present Protocol shall not enter into force until the Chairman of the Committee referred to in the Preamble is satisfied that there has been concluded between the Government of Liberia and the Finance Corporation of America an adequate arrangement for financing the Plan of Assistance on the lines indicated in the annexed report of Mr. Ligthart.

3. Subject to the provisions of paragraph 2, the present Protocol shall enter into force as soon as the Government of Liberia has deposited with the Secretary-General of the League of Nations:

i) a declaration signed by the President of the Republic certifying that a law has been enacted or other necessary measures have been taken so as to satisfy the requirements of Article 22 together with a certified true copy of such legislation as has been enacted;

ii) the instrument of ratification of the present Protocol,

or has notified the Secretary-General through diplomatic channels that the said two instruments have been despatched.

4. If the Protocol has not entered into force by _____ its entry into force shall require the consent of the Council of the League of Nations.

DONE at _____ on _____ 1933, in a single copy which shall remain deposited in the archives of the League of Nations and of which a certified true copy shall be delivered by the Secretary-General to the Government of Liberia. In faith whereof the undersigned has signed the present Protocol.

Annex to the Draft Protocol establishing a Plan of Assistance for Liberia

MR. LIGTHART'S REPORT REFERRED TO IN THE PROTOCOL.[19]

1. At its meeting on May 19th, 1933, the Council Committee decided to take advantage of the presence in Europe of special representatives of the Liberian Government, the Finance Corporation of America, and the Firestone Plantations Company, in order to settle the financial questions left open in the scheme drawn up by the Committee (document C.720.1932.VII.) It was suggested that the delegate of the Liberian Government and the representatives of the American groups concerned should begin negotiations as soon as possible, and I was asked to take charge of these negotiations, in collaboration with the Secretariat of the League of Nations.

2. We met in London from June 8th to June 23rd, 1933. The Liberian Government was represented by Mr. Grimes, Secretary of State, and Baron de Lynden, Chargé d'Affaires in London; the Finance Corporation of America by its Vice-President, Mr. L. T. Lyle, and the Firestone Interests by Mr. Harvey Firestone, Jr.

The special representative of the United States Government, General Blanton Winship, has closely followed our proceedings throughout.

I was greatly helped by the presence of Dr. Mackenzie, with whom M. Brunot and I visited Liberia in 1931 and who went there again in 1932.

In drawing up the present report, I have had the opportunity of consulting the Financial Section of the Secretariat of the League of Nations from time to time.

3. In the first instance, we dealt with the *minimum budget* required by the Liberian Government for its ordinary running expenses. In this connection we discussed the actual budget in

---

[19]This report reproduces the essential conclusions reached by Mr. Ligthart in the more comprehensive report on his investigations which he presented to the Committee appointed by the Council to examine the problem raised by the Liberian Government's request for assistance (Document C./Liberia 39 and C./Liberia 39 (a)).

application in Liberia for 1933, although this budget is not one sanctioned by the Financial Adviser. This budget totals Lib. $367,800,[12] whereas the estimates worked out by the Finance Corporation provide only for Lib. $281,500.[13]

After careful consideration, I came to the conclusion that the figures of Lib. $300,000[13] a year is sufficient to defray the running expenses of the Liberian Government. My figure is rather higher than that proposed by the Finance Corporation and that suggested in the experts' report (document C.469.M.238.1932, page 26). This is on the assumption that every possible saving in the budget will, of course, be made.[14]

4. Salaries and expenses for *loan officials* total about Lib. $44,500, as given by the Finance Corporation, and Bank of Commission charges Lib. $7,500.

5. We have also considered the *cost of the plan of assistance,* and I have reached the conclusion that about $150,000 a year are needed in order to carry out the plan of assistance. This sum includes salaries and travelling expenses to Europe to the amount of U. S. $78,000, the balance being for roads, bridges, public health, etc. (for further particulars, see paragraph 19).[15]

The salaries and conditions of service of the foreign League officials are to be those obtaining for white officials of similar rank serving in West Africa, and making allowance for the temporary character of the appointment.

6. We then took up the questions of *arrears apart from the loan*. In view of the difficult financial position of Liberia, I think that the creditors must make a sacrifice at least of interest on their claims. The first step is to fix the amount of the outstanding claims. I estimate that these total about Lib. $500,-000. It seems to me that a provision of a sum not exceeding Lib. $40,000 per annum in the Liberian budget would be a fair settlement for the amortisation of these claims. The details of the funding arrangements to be made with the creditors on these

[12]Exclusive of salaries and expenses for loan officials and of arrears.

[14]The Liberian Delegation wished that the minimum budget figure of Lib. $300,000 a year should be raised to Lib. $375,000. This amendment has not been retained by the Committee.

[15]The Liberian Government considers that the sum of $150,000 a year for the plan of assistance is excessive.
The Committee does not agree with this view.

lines should be left to the Liberian Government and the Chief Adviser in consultation with the Financial Adviser.[16]

7. With regard to the *interest rate on the loan,* the Finance Corporation is prepared to reduce this from 7 per cent to 5 per cent. The interest charge would therefore be in future about U.S. $125,000[17] per annum instead of U.S. $175,000. Amortisation will require an additional U.S. $66,000 per annum. Outstanding interest on the loan amounted, on January 1st, 1933, to U.S. $133,000. The Finance Corporation proposes to take up this amount in additional bonds.

8. Funds for the following items have therefore to be provided:

	$	$	$
(1) Running Government expenses (estimates for the first year)		300,000	
(2) Execution of plan of assistance	150,000		
Salaries and expenses for loan officials	44,500		
Bank Commission charges ...	7,500		
		202,000	
(3) Interest on loan		125,000	
			627,000
(4) Amortisation of arrears		40,000	
(5) Amortisation of loan		66,000	
			106,000
Total			$733,000

9. Estimates for *revenues* of the fiscal year 1933 total about Lib. $456,500.

I am confident that this amount will be increased considerably by the application of the plan and by a proper administration, as this will lead to a speedy development of the country and its resources.

[16]The Liberian Government makes a reservation as regards the question of arrears, as this amount is already provided for by act of the legislature in internal bonds.
The Committee did not feel able to give effect to this reservation.
[17]Anticipating the issue of further bonds.

For the time being we have, however, to face an adverse balance in the budget and to make the necessary provisions to meet this. In this connection it should be borne in mind that the cost of the plan of assistance for the first year will be less than that estimated, as it is proposed that the plan should come into operation gradually.

10. First of all, it is necessary to guarantee that sufficient funds for the salaries of the foreign officials, and other expenses provided for in the plan of assistance, will be available.

I therefore propose that the Finance Corporation, by the issue of fresh bonds, should provide an initial fund of U.S. $150,000 as *working capital* for the operation of the plan; that the amounts withdrawn from this fund should, if possible, be repaid to it out of the Liberian budget; and that, if such replenishment is not possible, the Finance Corporation should in any event by the issue of bonds ensure that the fund shall always be in a position to pay salaries and travelling expenses to Europe of the foreign experts provided for in the plan, estimated at U.S. $78,000 per annum.

Out of this fund should be paid the cost of the plan of assistance, and, in the first place, the salaries of the new foreign officials.

The fund will be paid in a special blocked account of the Liberian Government into a bank to be determined later by the Council committee. The Council committee will equally have to decide the conditions under which the fund has to be administered.[18]

11. Under my scheme *priority* is therefore as follows:

(a) Ordinary running expenses of the Government (estimates for the first year)   Lib. $300,000
(b) Cost of the plan of assistance, salaries and expenses of loan officials .... U.S. $78,000
    Bank commission charges .... Lib. $124,000
(c) Interest on loan .... U.S. $125,000

[18]The Liberian Government reiterates the reservation it made in May 1932 to the effect that it could not possibly accept a new loan issued under new external bonds.
The Committee thought it essential to issue the relatively small amount necessary to guarantee the salaries of the foreign experts.

(d) Remaining balance:
   One-half to be proportionately allocated:
   To amortisation of arrears of internal
      debt to an amount not exceeding ..... Lib. $40,000
   To amortisation of the loan .... U.S. $66,000
   The other half to be devoted to the develop-
   ment of the country.

If the *annual interest* on the loan cannot be met out of revenue, it is to be renounced at the end of the corresponding fiscal year.

12. The question of *transferring funds* from Liberia abroad will probably only arise in respect to a portion of the foreign officials' salaries, but it will clearly be the duty of the Government of Liberia, the Chief Adviser, and the Financial Adviser to maintain sufficient bullion in the country for the proper operation of the currency.

13. The figures upon which the plan of assistance is based must be subject to reconsideration, at the moment when the plan is brought into force, in the light of the relative values of the currencies concerned at that time and possibly their future prospects. In particular, it is essential that the arrangements made as regards providing and replenishing the working capital fund should be adequate to permit offering conditions of service sufficient to enable suitable foreign experts to be engaged. At present, it is impossible to say what, at any particular moment in the future, will be the relation between the United States dollar and the Liberian dollar, or the gold value of either currency. Accordingly, wherever in the present report a table had to be drawn up showing expenditure both in United States dollars and Liberian dollars, I have treated the United States dollar and the Liberian dollar as equivalent to one another, as they originally were.

14. I have not thought it my duty to consider the merits of the existing loan contract, but have contented myself to find within the given limits of the situation the best solutions for all parties concerned.

Permanent modifications in the Loan Agreement have been discussed independently by the Liberian Government and the Finance Corporation.

A special arrangement is also being made to modify the new loan contract temporarily, so as to bring its provisions into line with the plan of assistance.[19]

15. The conditions on which the Finance Corporation is willing to accept my proposals, including the renunciation of interest and the provision of fresh capital, as stated to the Council Committee at its meeting on June 27th, 1933, as follows:

"(a) That Liberia accept and approve by legislative action the proposed supplementary agreement to the Loan Agreement of 1926[20] and remove all legislative acts and executive orders in contravention of the Loan Agreement of 1926.

"(b) That Liberia accept and approve, by legislative action where necessary, the programme of assistance as recommended by the Council Committee on Liberia to the Council of the League of Nations, including the recommendations contained in Mr. Ligthart's report to the Committee.

"(c) That Liberia recognise the existing Depository Agreement between the Liberian Government and the United States Trading Company Banking Department, and function in accordance with this agreement.

"(d) That Liberia concur in Mr. Ligthart's recommendation that the floating indebtedness be gradually amortised from current revenues without recourse to the issuance of 3 per cent internal bonds.'"[19]

16. In regard to the Plantation Contract, I understand from the Firestone Plantations Company's representative that it is prepared to make the utmost possible allowance for the general interests of Liberia, and that it would be perfectly ready, in consideration of the well-being of the population, to take account of competent opinions. In particular, I understand that

[19]The Liberian Government would hope for further reformation of the two contracts with the Finance Corporation of America and the Firestone Plantations Company respectively.

The Committee was of opinion that the question of permanent modifications in these contracts is a matter for negotiations between the parties concerned.

[20]The text of this agreement was reproduced in League Document C.421.M.214.1933. VII, June 27, 1933.

the Firestone Plantations Company, during the operation of the plan, will be glad to consult with the Chief Adviser and the Provincial Commissioner concerned in the selection of additional land.[19]

17. If the plan is adopted, I must emphasise the importance of having an undertaking from the Liberian Government that it will submit to the Chief Adviser any proposals that may be made by prospective concessionaires and to give due consideration to any advice he may offer, without, however, undertaking to bind itself by such advice.

18. As a preliminary stage it was necessary to fix the amount of the Liberian budget, and for convenience only I have considered the items of the separate departments of the Government. It is clear, however, that, broadly speaking, the total sum of the budget in proportion to the revenues of Liberia is of more importance than the detailed application of the sums available for the various departments. I anticipate that the details of the amount to be allocated to the individual departments will be considered by the Chief Adviser in consultation with the Liberian Government and the Financial Adviser.[21]

19. A detailed estimate for the plan of assistance is given below. It will be seen that the number of staff proposed is that agreed to by the Liberian Government and the Committee. It should be noted, however, that provision is made for two doctors, whereas it was decided that, in the first instance, one doctor only should be appointed, the second post being filled when, in the opinion of the Chief Adviser, funds permitted of this.

It is clear that it is impossible to define a figure for the first year of the working of the plan. My figure represents, there-

[21]The Government of Liberia fears that no provision for education is made in the annual budget, and that the schools of the country will be limited to those provided by sundry missionary boards. As this would stagnate the intellectual, spiritual and cultural development of the youth of the country, it finds it impossible to agree to the budget proposed.

The Committee, emphasising the importance of education, felt that this question must be left to be decided by the Liberian Government on the advice of the Chief Adviser and the Financial Adviser.

fore, the cost of the plan as adopted when all the appointments
have been made.

	U.S. $
Chief Adviser	12,000
Three Commissioners at $8,000 each	24,000
Three assistants at $6,000 each	18,000
Two doctors at $8,000 each	16,000
Travelling expenses	8,000

——— U.S. $78,000[22]

	Lib. $
Sanitation	10,000
Road construction	54,000
Education medical assistants	3,000
Unforeseen	5,000

——— Lib. $72,000

Approximate total $150,000
(Signed)   TH. LIGTHART.

LEAGUE OF NATIONS

C.596.1933.VII.
GENEVA, *October 14th, 1933.*

REQUEST FOR ASSISTANCE SUBMITTED BY THE LIBERIAN GOVERNMENT.

REPORT BY THE REPRESENTATIVE OF POLAND.

My colleagues have before them the final report of the Committee appointed by the Council in January 24th, 1931, to consider the problem raised by the Liberian request for assistance.

I need not recall the history of this request, with which my
colleagues are fully conversant, nor go into the details of the
proposals that our Committee has put before us in the form
of a draft Protocol to be adopted at a later stage by the Council and to be signed and ratified by the Liberian Government.

[22]The Liberian Government thinks that the salaries provided for
the foreign advisers are too high.
The Committee did not agree with this view.

The draft Protocol deals both with the financial and the administrative aspects of the problem.

I ought however to draw attention to certain points of particular importance.

Under the plan certain duties fall to the Council. It will be remembered that in May 1932 the Council saw no objection in principle to undertaking them provided that the plan was accepted by all concerned.

In October 1932 the Committee unanimously adopted general principles for a draft plan. These were accepted by the Liberian Government, conditionally on a satisfactory outcome of the financial negotiations to be undertaken between the Liberian Government and the Finance Corporation of America. The proposals resulting from the negotiations (in which the Liberian Government was assisted by the Financial Expert, Mr. Ligthart, and the Financial Section of the Secretariat), are included in the Plan before us to-day. The administrative clauses of the Plan are substantially the same as those contained in the general principles prepared in October 1932.

It must be pointed out, moreover, that the Committee agreed unanimously that the Chief Adviser provided for in the Plan ought not to be of the same nationality as the Financial Adviser, nor should he be of the nationality of any country which had territory adjacent to Liberia. My colleagues will probably associate themselves with this view.

The question raised by the Liberian Government as to the nationality of the Chief Adviser is thus answered, and I suppose that the Liberian representative will agree that we need not discuss the matter further.

The proposals now before us represent the considered view of those members of the Council which are represented on the Committee as well as of the United States of America which is also so represented. I trust that it may be possible for the Council to express their agreement with this view. In any case I suggest that the Plan of Assistance should be sent by the Secretary-General to the Liberian Government with a request that between now and our next session it will inform the Council whether it wishes to accept the assistance of the League on the terms proposed in the present Plan. I am informed that the Liberian Legislature is at present in session and that it will therefore be possible for the Liberian Government to give an early reply.

The problem raised by the Liberian Government's request for assistance has engaged the attention of the Council for nearly three years and has been very carefully examined. The time seems now to have come when a conclusion should be reached. My colleagues will in this connection note that the Committee stated in its report that the present Plan represented the considered conditions upon which assistance could, in the opinion of the Committee, be granted to Liberia, and that the Plan as it stands must be taken as a whole.

The Council will undoubtedly wish to express its gratitude to the Committee, and above all its President, for their labours and to associate itself in the Committee's expression of appreciation of the work done by the Experts, M. Brunot, now Governor of the Tchad Territory, Mr. Ligthart and Dr. Mackenzie.

LEAGUE OF NATIONS

C/Liberia 41.
GENEVA, *October 9th, 1933.*

REQUEST FOR ASSISTANCE SUBMITTED BY THE GOVERNMENT OF LIBERIA.

NOTE BY THE SECRETARY-GENERAL.

At the request of the Representative of the United States of America the Secretary-General has the honour to communicate to the Members of the Committee the following memorandum, of which a short summary was presented to the Committee at to-day's meeting.

OCTOBER 9th, 1933.
Statement submitted by the American Representative on the Liberian Committee of the Council

On February 7, 1933, the Liberian Secretary of State submitted a lengthy memorandum (League Document C/Liberia /34, February 28, 1933) making certain allegations with respect to the establishment and operation of the Finance Corporation of America Loan of 1926. The following June, Mr. Grimes submitted a further document consisting of a letter prepared by K. Jefferies Adorkor, Jr., a Liberian in the Bureau of Audit, concerning the expenditure of approximately $156,000. of the proceeds of the Finance Corporation Loan. Following the adoption on June 27, 1933, by the Council Committee on Liberia of the Revised League Plan of Assistance and Mr. Ligthart's report, Mr. Grimes submitted a third statement (included in League document No. C.421.M.214./1933.VII).

Aside from certain statements in the document last mentioned, which relate exclusively to his opposition to the Revised League Plan, Mr. Grimes' main contentions are as follows:

1. That in 1926 Liberia "did not desire a loan, either for financial or economic rehabilitation, or any other existing necessity" (Document of February 7, 1933), but that its "reluctant" acceptance was forced on Liberia by Firestone interests.

2. That "a large proportion of the amount of the Loan was misspent and even thrown away, without any benefit to Liberia . . ." (Par. 3, Memorandum annexed to Revised League Plan dated June 27, 1933).

3. That the present economic condition of Liberia is due to the existence of the Finance Corporation Loan of 1926 and to the bad judgement or incompetence of the advisership officials appointed thereunder.

The American Representative has carefully examined the statements made or sponsored by Mr. Grimes, and in many instances he has been able to check his allegations with the original records. The American Representative finds Mr. Grimes' statements inaccurate and misleading, and his conclusions without foundation. A detailed statement in connection with Mr. Grimes' contentions is being submitted for the information of the Committee. It is shown therein:

1. That Liberia sought the Finance Corporation loan for the following reasons:

    a. In order to liquidate the internal and floating debts, which had risen to over $600,000., and

    b. In order to relieve Liberia of the Customs Receivership established under the 1912 Loan.

Both of these objectives were realized under the Finance Corporation Loan Agreement.

The American Government concerned itself in the Loan to the extent of extending good offices during preliminary discussions, and of intimating that, should Liberia so request, the American Government would be willing to assume certain clearly defined functions with respect to arbitration and the designation of Loan officials. The American Government did not induce American capital to invest in the Loan, nor did it assume responsibility for its security.

2. Over ninety percent of the proceeds of the bonds issued under the Finance Corporation Loan went to retire prior obligations of Liberia. That less than ten percent was utilized for other purposes, was due to Liberia's early violations of the Loan Agreement and to the refusal of the Liberian Government satisfactorily to settle these matters. Had they been settled, further funds would have been made available for general purposes.

Mr. De La Rue, first Financial Adviser under the Loan, had to do with the expenditure of only approximately $50,000. from Loan funds, and not $156,000. as alleged in a Liberian statement. The question of Mr. De La Rue's judgement in this matter is one of opinion.

3. The foreign officials serving Liberia under the Finance Corporation Loan Agreement have been men of character, experience and proven ability. They have given the Liberian Government constructive advice on repeated occasions. Among other matters, they have advised the Liberian Government regarding:

Waste of public funds in the maintenance of overstaffed or unnecessary institutions and bureaux; failure of the Government to enforce the payment of delinquent taxes; failure of the Government to prosecute Liberian officials for embezzlement, or to take action against them under their bonds; failure of the Government to enforce the payment into the Treasury of Consular and other fees; failure of the Government to foster or encourage commerce, or to open the hinterland to trade; failure of the Government to interest itself in the condition of the million and a half native peoples, or to utilize the taxes collected from the natives for their benefit.

The advice and recommendations of the foreign officials appointed under the Finance Corporation Loan Agreement have been met with opposition or indifference on the part of the Liberian Government. The failure of the Government to act is responsible for the conditions which exist in Liberia at present.

The unwillingness of the Liberian Government to accept competent advice has not been confined to the relations of the Government with the various American advisers appointed under the Loan Agreement, or previously. The majority of the recommendations of the 1930 Commission of Inquiry do not appear to have been put into effect, and the recommendations made to Liberia by the experts appointed under the auspices of the League of Nations since 1931, have been opposed.

OCTOBER 9, 1933.

Detailed Statement submitted by the American Representative on the Council Committee on Liberia, concerning certain allegations made by the Liberian Secretary of State.

Enclosed with the Statement are the following documents:

1. Statement submitted on June 23, 1933, to the Council Committee, by Mr. Harvey S. Firestone, Jr.
2. Copy of letter dated June 14, 1930, from the Finance Corporation of America to the Liberian Government.
3. Copy of Liberian reply to above letter, dated October 1, 1930.
4. List of 31 separate recommendations made to the Liberian Government by the Financial Adviser between 1929 and 1932, with a notation describing the action taken, if any.
5. List of fifteen recent incorrect statements made by Mr. Grimes, together with corrections.
6. List of Liberian officials and employees, together with amounts received from the Liberian Government in 1932.

On February 7, 1933, the Liberian Secretary of State submitted a lengthy memorandum (League Document C/Liberia

/34, February 28, 1933) making certain allegations with respect to the establishment and operation of the Finance Corporation of America Loan of 1926. The following June, Mr. Grimes submitted a further document consisting of a letter prepared by K. Jefferies Adorkor, Jr., a Liberian in the Bureau of Audit, concerning the expenditure of approximately $156,000 of the proceeds of the Finance Corporation Loan. Following the adoption on June 27, 1933 by the Council Committee on Liberia of the Revised League Plan of Assistance and Mr. Ligthart's report, Mr. Grimes submitted a third statement (included in League Document No. C.421.M.214/1933—VII).

Aside from certain statements in the document last mentioned, which relate exclusively to his opposition to the Revised League Plan, Mr. Grimes' main contentions are as follows:

1. That in 1926 Liberia "did not desire a loan, either for financial or economic rehabilitation, or any other existing necessity" (Document of February 7, 1933), but that its "reluctant" acceptance was forced on Liberia by Firestone interests.

2. That "a large proportion of the amount of the Loan was misspent and even thrown away, without any benefit to Liberia . . ." (Par. 3, Memorandum annexed to Revised League Plan dated June 27, 1933).

3. That the present economic condition of Liberia is due to the existence of the Finance Corporation Loan of 1926 and to the bad judgement or incompetence of the advisership officials appointed thereunder.

The American Representative has examined in detail the statements made or sponsored by Mr. Grimes, and in many instances had been able to check his allegations with the original records. The American Representative finds Mr. Grimes' statements inaccurate and misleading, and his conclusions without foundation. Mr. Grimes' contentions are discussed in detail hereafter:

1. Mr. Grimes alleges that in 1926 Liberia "did not desire a loan, either for financial or economic rehabilitation, or any other existing necessity," but that its "reluctant" acceptance was forced on Liberia by Firestone interests.

The following quotation from the Report of the Experts (Brunot, Ligthart and Mackenzie, who investigated Liberia in

June–July 1931 under the auspices of the League Committee on Liberia, indicates a contrary view:

"During the war, Liberia received from the United States an advance of $35,000 which proved quite insufficient to tide the Republic over its financial difficulties. These difficulties are clearly revealed in the text of the Acts of August 17th, 1917, February 5th, 1918, January 20th, 1923, and February 5th, 1925, copies of which are annexed to the present document. The purpose of these Acts was the forced funding of all the internal floating debts by the payment of arrears on these debts, in the first place by means of 3 percent bonds redeemable in twelve years, then by 3 percent bonds redeemable in twenty years, and lastly by 5 percent bonds redeemable in thirty-five years.

"This method of meeting current difficulties was no novelty for Liberia, having already been utilized in 1912. On that occasion, it was accompanied by a reduction of one-third in the salaries of officials, and resulted in the redemption of a sum of $198,763.54 of debts falling due immediately by means of 3 percent bonds repayable in twenty years.

"There can be no doubt that this method of meeting immediate and pressing needs is attractive from the point of view of the Government; but it cannot be justified unless provision is made in advance for the payment of interest and redemption during the ensuing years without fresh floating debts being contracted. *This latter point is always lost sight of in Liberia,* and, since the last Funding Act February 5th, 1925, the floating debt has again steadily increased and the chronic trouble from which the administration suffers—i.e., the accumulation of arrears on the salaries of officials—has again been seriously felt. *Difficulties grew more and more serious, and the Government naturally bethought itself again of the old solution, the conclusion of a new loan to get rid for a short time of the most pressing demands.*"

There were two primary reasons, which Mr. Grimes ignores, that impelled the Liberian Government to seek the Finance Corporation Loan.

President Barclay who, as Secretary of State, negotiated the 1926 Loan, who initialled the preliminary draft on behalf of

his Government in New York City on September 17, 1925, and
who subsequently supported the ratification of the Loan by the
Liberian Congress, stated to General Winship in May 1933
that the two reasons the Liberian Government desired the loan
were:

1. To pay off the internal and floating debts which had
   risen to over $600,000 and
2. To relieve Liberia of the Customs Receivership established under the 1912 loan.

Both of these objectives were realized by the Loan Agreement of 1926. Moreover, in comparison with the rates on which
other foreign issues were underwritten in that period, the terms
of the Finance Corporation Loan were distinctly favourable to
Liberia.[23]

The Firestone interests recommended the acceptance of a
loan by Liberia. They were of the opinion that the proceeds of
a loan, if utilized in the proper way, would promote the general development of the country and in this sense contribute to
the successful prosecution of the company's main interest,—
the plantation project. There is likewise evidence that Mr.
Firestone shared the widespread American interest in the
progress of Liberia, and that, entirely aside from his business
concerns, he wished to see the country develop along sound
economic and social lines.[24] There is no evidence that, when the
matter of a Liberian loan was first considered, the Firestone
organization itself had any interest in financing such an issue.
The Firestone Company desired, on the contrary, that such a
loan should be made by the American Government, and included a paragraph (k) in the original draft of the Plantation
Agreement to this effect.

[23]The Finance Corporation Loan of 1926 to Liberia was 7%, issued to the Government at 90. On November 1, 1926, the Kingdom
of Belgium floated a $100,000,000 Loan, at 7%, issued *to the public*
at 94. The Liberian Loan is callable at 102; the Belgian loan is
callable at 105.

During this general period Government loans *at 7% or above*
were contracted by Argentine, Bolivia, France, Yugoslavia, Peru
and Poland.

[24]Enclosure 1. Statement submitted on June 23, 1933 to the Council Committee on Liberia, by Mr. Harvey S. Firestone, Jr.

This draft was submitted to the Secretary of State (Mr. Hughes) in a letter from Mr. Firestone dated December 10, 1924. Mr. Hughes replied, under date of December 22, 1924, stating (with reference to paragraph (k)) that

"In this connection, it should be clearly understood that this statement in the contract . . . must not be taken by the Government of Liberia or in any other quarter to mean that I intend to reopen the question of a government loan or that any committal in this respect is involved."

The American Government concerned itself with the Finance Corporation Loan to the extent of extending good offices during preliminary discussions, and of intimating that it would be willing to assume certain clearly defined functions with respect to arbitration and the designation of loan officials. In response to the request of Liberia it later agreed to assume these functions.

The American Government neither induced American capital to invest in the Loan, nor did it assume responsibility for its security. This was recognized by President King[25] at the time and on October 18, 1928, he referred to the Loan in the following terms:

"It has also been suggested that the Liberian Government was coerced by the United States Department of State in making the Firestone Rubber Agreement and the obtaining of the 7% Gold Loan of 1927 . . .

"Knowing these charges to be absolutely untrue, I felt it a

[25]By reproducing a series of alleged telegrams said to have been exchanged between Messrs. De La Rue and Bussell, American citizens acting as officials in the Liberian Receivership under the 1912 Loan, Mr. Grimes endeavours to create the impression that President King participated in confidential negotiations with Mr. Firestone in 1926, the purport of which negotiations were never divulged to a "responsible official of Liberia." (Memorandum of February 7, 1933, page 17).

President King was not in Europe at any time during the year 1926. Mr. King left Monrovia in May 1927, which was five months after the ratification by the Liberian Legislature of the completed Loan Agreement. He states that during his absence he did not see either Mr. Firestone or Mr. Firestone, Jr., in Paris or elsewhere.

duty we owe not only to the United States Government but to ourselves to make a public denial of them.

"The presence of American assistance in the financial administration of Liberian affairs was not unsolicited, but rather a realization of the desires of the people of Liberia . . .

"The American Government during the whole period of its unbroken friendly intercourse with Liberia, has never sought any special political right or economic privilege for itself or its citizens; but rather, has always stood four square in the 'open door policy' of equal opportunity and equal treatment by Liberia to all foreign nations.

"Therefore, as long as we maintain our reputation for orderly government and continue to show a decent regard and respect for our international engagements, I see no reasonable grounds for apprehensions and fears as to Liberia's future, safety and security."

2. Mr. Grimes alleges that "a large proportion of the amount of the loan was misspent and even thrown away, without any benefit to Liberia, by agents appointed to serve as Financial Adviser and under the Financial Adviser . . ."

The Finance Corporation Loan netted the Liberian Government $2,027,700. Over ninety percent of this amount was used to retire Liberia's prior existing obligations,[26] and less than ten percent ($168,169.73) was used for other purposes, as follows:

Sanitation: $11,730.39, or 0.58% of $2,027,700.
Public Works: $156,439.34, or 7.72% of $2,027,700.

---

[26]A total of $1,859,530.27, or 91.7% of the proceeds of the Finance Corporation Loan, was expended as follows: (See also figures appearing on page 30 of League Document C.469.M.238.1932. VII).

Redemption of 1912 external bonds, and expenses in connection therewith	$1,180,669.27
Legal fees, printing, etc.	22,350.57
Repayment of debt to U.S. Government	35,610.46
To extinguish Liberian internal debt	175,085.84
To extinguish Liberian floating debt (for breakdown of this total, see page 30, League Document referred to above)	431,149.09
Cash balance on hand, Dec. 31, 1930	14,665.04
Total (91.7% of $2,027,700)	$1,859,530.27

With respect to *sanitation,* the urgent desirability of which was recognized in the Preamble (item e) of the Loan Agreement, it is pertinent to recall that following the yellow fever epidemic of 1929, which caused the death of the American Minister and of the Educational Adviser to Liberia as well as numerous other foreigners, and as a result of representations thereafter made to Liberia by the American and other Governments, arrangements were concluded for the loan to Liberia of Surgeon Howard F. Smith of the United States Public Health Service. Dr. Smith reached Monrovia early in 1930, and was withdrawn by the American Government eleven months later. The following communication, outlining the reasons for his recall, was submitted to the official acting as Liberian Secretary of State by the American Chargé d'Affaires on December 12, 1930:

LEGATION OF THE UNITED STATES OF AMERICA.
Monrovia, Liberia, December 12, 1930.
S. DAVID COLEMAN, ESQUIRE,
  Department of State,
        Monrovia.
SIR,
I have been instructed to inform you that in view of the failure of the Liberian Government to support measures in favour of sanitation and public health recommended by Surgeon Howard F. Smith of the United States Public Health Service who was loaned to Liberia to act as Chief Medical Adviser to that country the American Government is obliged to conclude that no useful purpose can be served by Dr. Smith's further presence in Liberia at this time, and that he has accordingly been directed to return to the United States.

Dr. Smith is a competent officer of wide practical experience and he has made every effort to bring to the Liberian Government a realization of the desirability of adopting and enforcing measures of sanitation for the protection of the lives of the Liberian people. Every support has been given to these efforts by the American Chargé d'Affaires ad interim acting upon repeated specific instructions from the American Government. Because of the lack of coöperation on the part of the Liberian Government and officials this work has been unproductive.

I am therefore instructed to make it clear to you that the responsibility for the dangers to which the Liberian people are being exposed must rest upon Liberia alone.

My Government desires me to state that the Government of Great Britain and of France[27] have been informed of the action which the American Government has been impelled to take with regard to Dr. Smith, and of the reasons therefor.

I am, Sir, with sentiments of highest esteem,

Very truly yours

SAMUEL REBER, JR.

With respect to *public works,* the Liberian Secretary of State under date of June 1933, submitted a statement (published as League Document No. C/Liberia/38) containing a series of allegations concerning the expenditure of approximately $156,000. from loan funds. This document was prepared by K. Jefferies Adorkor, Jr., a Liberian at present illegally serving in the Bureau of Audit.[28]

The facts concerning the utilization of the above $156,000 are as follows:

The Loan Agreement of 1926 became operative on July 1st, 1927. From that date until January 31st, 1928, public works were under the direction of President King. On January 31st, 1928, a Department of Public Works was created. This Department functioned from then until its abolition on December 31st, 1930, under a Liberian official, as Director of Public Works.

Mr. De La Rue became Financial Adviser on July 1st, 1927. He did not return to Monrovia to assume his functions there until October 1st, 1927. From October 1st, 1927, until January 4th, 1928, public works were temporarily under the general supervision of Mr. De La Rue, subject to President King's directions.

The total amount spent on public works from July 1st, 1927, to December 31st, 1930 (the date on which the Public Works

[27]The above communication was also transmitted to the German Government.

[28]Mr. Adorkor, formerly an accountant for a British commercial firm in Monrovia, was tried and convicted of forgery in 1925. This conviction was later set aside by the Supreme Court.

Department was abolished) was approximately $535,000 of which approximately $156,000 came from Loan funds, and the balance from general revenues.

According to the present Acting Financial Adviser, no loan funds as such were available for disbursement in Monrovia for public works until March 29th, 1928, nearly two months after Mr. De La Rue's final departure from Monrovia because of illness.[29] From July 1st, 1927 until January 4th, 1928 (on which date Mr. De La Rue was taken ill), a total of slightly over $50,000 was expended under President King's directions, and subject to Mr. De La Rue's general supervision. This amount was obtained through a special credit established in New York City in anticipation of Loan Funds and it was paid off on January 3rd, 1928, when $63,000 derived from the sale of bonds was made available in New York under Article XI, Section 7, of the Loan Agreement of 1926.

The amount of approximately $50,000 was apparently the only funds for public works ultimately met from the Loan, with which Mr. De La Rue had any connection whatever, *and not $156,000, as stated by Mr. Adorkor.*

This amount of approximately $50,000 was expended principally for the purchase in the United States of equipment and supplies, and in many of these transactions Mr. De La Rue conducted the arrangements. This was for the convenience of the Liberian Government but only upon specific instructions, which were issued by President King.

The public utilities recommended by Mr. De La Rue appear to have been rather modest in character and relatively inexpensive. They represented equipment regarded as essential, and the existence of which is in fact taken for granted, in practically any community.

Mr. Adorkor has adduced no proof that the materials and equipment were not of good quality, or not purchased at the

[29]Following his resignation as Financial Adviser to Liberia, Mr. De Le Rue was appointed Financial Adviser-General Receiver of the Republic of Haiti, whose annual budget averages ten times the amount of the Liberian budget. The Special Commission which investigated Haitian conditions in 1930 characterized the financial achievement of this administration as "noteworthy."

Mr. De Le Rue still holds the position of Financial Adviser-General Receiver in Haiti.

lowest prices obtainable. On the contrary, there is evidence that, by arranging on behalf of the Liberian Government to place various orders direct, Mr. De La Rue was able to save the Government money which it would otherwise have had to pay in commission, bank charges, etcetera.[30]

The contracts of all the engineers serving the Liberian Government were made by the Liberian Government and not by the American Fiscal officials. The qualifications and recommendations in connection with candidates were customarily submitted through the fiscal officials, but the decisions in respect to employment were made by the Liberian Government. No proof has been submitted by Mr. Adorkor that these men were not technically competent.[31]

The installations completed, and the equipment purchased in connection therewith, functioned throughout the period prior to the establishment of a separate Department of Public Works under Liberian administration on January 31, 1928. According to Mr. De La Rue, the radio service, as a case in point, showed a profit to the Liberian Government during the time it was under his general supervision. Subsequently under Liberian management it has consistently been operated at a loss and a later Financial Adviser repeatedly recommended that it be either closed down or turned over to a private company.

[30]For example, during Mr. De La Rue's absence from Liberia in 1927, the Liberian Government desired to take over the electric light plant ordered for Monrovia by a private Liberian purchaser who on arrival of the equipment was unable to pay the bill. Mr. De La Rue, who was in the United States, was instructed by cable to arrange the matter with the Westinghouse Company. He was able to obtain a 15% reduction, and the Company assumed all bank charges and interest.

[31]Mr. Adorkor's reference to one of the engineers (Mr. Kob) endeavours to create the impression that although Mr. Kob was endorsed by Mr. De La Rue as an engineer, his training had in fact been in "husbandry." Mr. Adorkor apparently bases this assumption on the fact that Mr. Kob had received training in the Colorado Agricultural College, although he does not state that the curriculum of this institution includes both electrical and irrigational engineering. Mr. Kob had been recommended by the Department of the Interior of the American Government. He had likewise been employed by the Denver and Rio Grande Railroad, and by the Installation Department of the Mountain States Telephone Company.

During the period between its establishment on January 31, 1928 and its abolition on December 31, 1930, there was expended by the Department of Public Works under the supervision and control of the Liberian Director of Public Works over $400,000 which included approximately $100,000 of the $156,000 derived from Loan funds. During this period the Liberian Treasury repeatedly transferred revenues to Loan fund accounts and Loan funds to revenue accounts without apparently making proper record of these transactions. It was not the duty of the Auditor functioning in the Financial Advisership under the Loan Agreement to keep these records and Mr. Adorkor is in error when he attempts to promote the inference that the Auditor was "embarrassed" by his inability to furnish information. The Loan Agreement merely provided against the withdrawal of funds from the Depositary except by check executed by the Secretary of the Treasury and approved by the Auditor, who first verified the intended withdrawal against the appropriation.[32]

From July 1, 1927 until the violation of the Loan Agreement by the Liberian Government at the end of 1932, this provision was enforced, but there was no check possible by the Fiscal Officials under the Loan Agreement over the expenditure of funds *after* they had been withdrawn from the Depositary and turned over to Liberian officials.

Control over the funds for public works during the period from January 31, 1928, to December 31, 1930 was in the hands of the Liberian Director of Public Works. All Loan funds for public works except approximately $50,000 (previously referred to, for purchases made abroad) were disbursed by this Liberian official. For the entire life of the Department of Public Works, Mr. Adorkor himself acted as its accountant and was therefore responsible for whatever system or lack of system that existed in this connection.

Much waste unquestionably occurred in the Department of Public Works. In this connection the League Experts who visited Liberia in 1931 stated:

". . . when the construction and improvement of the Monrovia-Kakata road was undertaken, large sums and considerable quan-

[32]See Loan Agreement: Article XII, paragraph 6.

tities of material were utilized for the building of private houses
in the capital. Where there is no supervision, wastage is bound
to occur." (League Document C.469.M.238, page 33.)

The installations and equipment, referred to in the statement prepared by Mr. Adorkor, were not ruined because they
were originally inferior in quality, but because of the treatment
which they received from Liberian operatives. Even to-day there
may still be seen along the Monrovia-Kakata road (sections of
which remain almost impassable because of the failure of the
Liberian Government to provide even the most elementary
maintenance) road machinery and equipment, reinforcing steel,
and unfinished cement work abandoned by the Department of
Public Works.

3. Mr. Grimes alleges that the present economic condition of
Liberia is due to the existence of the Finance Corporation Loan,
and to the bad judgment or incompetence of the advisership officials appointed thereunder.

Over ninety per cent of the funds derived from the Finance
Corporation Loan was used to retire Liberia's prior debts. By
the terms of the Loan Agreement (Article XV) Liberia agreed
that thereafter "no floating debt shall be created," and the
Financial Adviser made repeated representations on this subject. Nevertheless the floating debt began almost immediately
to mount and as of December 31, 1932, it stood at approximately $675,000.[33]

Among the causes for the growth of the floating debt, in no

[33]A legislative enactment, in violation of Article XV of the Loan
Agreement of 1926, was made by the Liberian Congress and approved by President Barclay in January 1933. This measure
authorized the issue of $650,000. in internal 3% bonds for the
ostensible purpose of funding the floating debt.

At the request of the Liberian Government, its fiscal position
was examined in detail by Mr. Th. Ligthart, financial expert of
the Liberian Committee of the Council of the League, in June 1933.
Mr. Ligthart recommended that the floating debt should gradually
be amortized from current revenues, without recourse to a bond
issue. (His report is published in League Document C.421.M.214;
see paragraph 6.)

Mr. Grimes has objected to this and other recommendations
made by the League financial expert of his own choice.

way connected with world economic conditions, may be mentioned the following:

Waste of public funds in the maintenance of over-staffed or unnecessary institutions and bureaux; failure of the Department of Justice to enforce payment of delinquent taxes; failure of the Department of Justice to prosecute Liberian officials for embezzlement or diversion of public funds and Government supplies, or to take action against them under their bonds; failure of the Liberian Government to enforce the payment into the Treasury of Consular and other fees; payments of funds due soldiers of the Frontier Force, whose money was collected by Liberian politicians and their friends; failure to institute reforms and economies repeatedly recommended by the Financial Adviser.[34]

On the other hand, the Liberian Government has done practically nothing to foster or encourage commerce, or to open the hinterland to trade, a "law" on the subject passed in 1930 to the contrary notwithstanding. No progress in the uplift of the native Liberian peoples has been seriously attempted by the Liberian Government,[35] nor have the taxes collected from the natives been spent for their benefit.

[34]The men serving the Liberian Government were of the highest character and ability. The majority of them (Messrs. Loomis, Mc-Caskey, Fitzsimmons and Homan) had all just previous to their Liberian appointments served with distinction in the financial mission in Persia. When they took over their duties there Persian finances were under a heavy deficit, and in three years this was converted into a revenue surplus, and there was sufficient cash in the treasury to pay off the entire funded debt of Persia.

Under their administration in Persia expenditures for public works increased from $100,000 to $2,500,000; for education from $700,000 to $1,500,000; and for public health from $120,000 to $275,000. Before coming to Liberia, a country whose largest budget in history amounted to less than $1,500,000, these officials had successfully handled Persian budgets in excess of $30,000,000 per annum.

[35]According to a statement prepared in May 1933 by the Advisory Committee on Education in Liberia (an organization composed of representatives of the various American mission boards and Colonization Societies) their total expenditures in Liberia have averaged approximately $250,000 a year. These contributions were made for educational, religious and physical development of the Liberian people, and constituted *more than four-fifths of the amount expended in Liberia for education.*

Commenting on conditions in Liberia in 1931, the experts sent out under the auspices of the League stated that there was:

". . . abundant proof that the governing class in Liberia has no idea how a state should use its financial resources . . ." (League Document No. C.469.M.238, page 33).

Less than ten per cent of the proceeds derived from Finance Corporation Loan funds was devoted to sanitation and public works. The experiences of the American Public Health official loaned to the Liberian Government in 1930 have already been described. Respecting public works, it was anticipated in the Loan Agreement that further sums would be released from time to time for this purpose.

Beginning in 1930, the Finance Corporation declined to make further advances available. Its reasons are contained in a lengthy letter, sent to the Liberian Government through the Fiscal Agent on June 14, 1930, in which nine specific violations of the Loan Agreement were listed, together with a statement to the effect that until these matters were satisfactorily adjusted, the Corporation would be compelled to withhold further advances.[36]

This communication is not a mere recital of complaints against the illegal actions of the Liberian Government; it contains helpful and constructive suggestions. It will be noted also that, notwithstanding the position taken by the Corporation against further advances for general purposes, it expressed its willingness to make a special advance totalling $18,000 for sanitation and for the Booker T. Washington Institute at Kakata.

The Liberian Government acknowledged the Finance Corporation letter of June 14, 1930, by a communication[37] signed by the President of Liberia on October 1, 1930, admitting the validity of most of the complaints listed by the company, and making assurances that thereafter the terms of the Loan Agreement would be complied with. They were not complied with, and the Corporation accordingly continued to withhold further advances.

To illustrate the type of recommendations submitted by the

[36]The full text of this document is submitted as Enclosure two.
[37]A copy of the Liberian reply is annexed as Enclosure three.

Financial Adviser in accordance with the terms of the Loan Agreement, a document (Enclosure 4) has been prepared from the original records. In it are listed thirty-one recommendations made to the Liberian Government between 1929 and 1932, together with a brief notation after each item regarding the action taken, if any. This list is by no means inclusive.

During the period covered by these recommendations, definite and concrete economies were effected in the offices functioning directly under the supervision of the Financial Adviser. The total cost of maintaining these offices was $127,294.00 in 1929; $106,510.00 in 1930; $92,770.00 in 1931; and $85,374.00 in 1932.

Mr. Grimes bases the arguments contained in his lengthy memorandum of February 7, 1933, on which many of his subsequent contentions appear to be based, on incorrect statements. A number of these have already been referred to. Fifteen others have been included in an annexed document (Enclosure 5), together with the pertinent corrections. This list is not inclusive.

ENCLOSURE ONE

STATEMENT SUBMITTED ON JUNE 23, 1933 TO THE COUNCIL COMMITTEE ON LIBERIA BY MR. HARVEY S. FIRESTONE, JR.

"Up to the present time we have invested more than $8,000,000 in Liberia and we have cleared and planted to rubber 53,087 acres on which there are approximately ten million rubber trees ranging in age from one to seven years. In due course a large proportion of these trees will be ready for tapping.

In the interests of health and sanitation we donated $20,000. to Harvard School of Tropical Medicine to aid in a research expedition in 1926 headed by Doctor Richard P. Strong of the Harvard School of Tropical Medicine and seven fellow-scientists, which made an extensive medical and biological survey of Liberia resulting in the most complete records yet compiled of the medical and social history of the people of Liberia and of all forms of life in West Africa.

A hospital has been erected at a cost of $56,000, and since our entry into Liberia we have spent an additional $200,000. in medical treatment resulting in greatly improved health for many thousands of Liberian people.

In 1927 a gift of $5,000. was made to the Harvard School of Tropical Medicine for the investigation of a preventive serum for yellow fever by Doctor A. W. Sellards.

We have contributed $6,500. for an anthropological survey by Doctor George Schwab of Peabody Museum of Harvard University which has resulted in an invaluable addition to the knowledge of the world regarding the background of the people of Liberia. In addition, we have spent approximately $25,000. on a motion picture expedition to Liberia, a large part of which forms a perpetual living record of the life and customs of the people of Liberia of this period.

We have donated $4,500. to the Yale School of Forestry to investigate and classify the woods of Liberia.

To help the natives of Liberia learn trades and become more useful citizens we established and operated a trade school and farm at a cost of $10,000. and retained the services of a famous German philologist for the preparation and publication of a grammar of the leading native language of Liberia, thereby putting this language into written form for the first time.

We have imported from the Far East and established in Liberia the highest yielding rubber stock in the world.

In order to provide reliable communications between Liberia, the United States and other countries we have established at a cost of $30,000. public radio service.

We undertook to provide Monrovia, the capital of Liberia, with a harbour and later, when it was found not practicable, we absorbed a loss of $115,000. sparing Liberia all expenses in connection with the undertaking.

We have expended $275,000. in the construction and maintenance of 125 miles of road within our plantations and in addition have contributed $65,000. to the extension and betterment of Government roads, which has materially aided the development of the interior of the country."

COPY OF A LETTER DATED JUNE 14, 1930 TRANSMITTED TO
THE LIBERIAN GOVERNMENT BY THE FINANCE CORPORATION
OF AMERICA THROUGH THE FISCAL AGENT.

"JUNE 14, 1930.

"THE NATIONAL CITY BANK OF NEW YORK,
   Fiscal Agent,
      New York, N. Y.

Under date of March 4, 1930 you transmitted to us the request of the Liberian Government that we take up $100,000 face value Liberian bonds on April 1, 1930. We replied on March 29 that we would take this request under advisement. As the owner of bonds of Liberia issued under the Loan Agreement dated September 1, 1926 between the Government of the Republic of Liberia and Finance Corporation of America, we have been seriously disturbed at the failure on the part of the Liberian Government to observe and carry into effect certain of the terms of such Agreement which vitally and detrimentally affects the security of the bonds, and unless adequate and appropriate measures are taken to restore the administration of the loan to its full effectiveness according to the purposes and terms of the Loan Agreement, Finance Corporation regrets that it must continue to hold under advisement the Government's request for our acceptance of delivery of bonds.

We have observed that:

1. The Government has refused to make payment of the salaries of the employees of the revenue service, both customs and internal from funds available and due such employees, in violation of the express terms of Section 1 of Article XIII of the Loan Agreement, and has notified the Financial Adviser that it proposes to continue to refuse to make such payments out of the specifically assigned revenues of the government in priority to payment of salaries to other employees of the Government not entitled to such priority under the express terms of Article XIII of the Loan Agreement.

2. The Government has failed to issue a certain Executive Order in the form and manner requested by the Financial Adviser pursuant to authority given by Article XII, paragraph 1

of the Loan Agreement and necessary to carry into effect rules and regulations governing the operation of the Fiscal Service.

3. The Government has failed to formally designate a depositary bank as provided in Article XVIII of the Loan Agreement.

4. The Secretary of State and the Secretary of the Treasury have failed to compel certain consular officers of the Government to submit an accounting of and pay consular fees into the treasury although their attention has been called to such delinquencies.

5. The Government has failed to diligently or effectively prosecute officers of the Fiscal Service for malfeasance in office, and has failed and refused to institute suit on the bonds of such officers to secure reimbursement of the financial loss so sustained by the Government in revenues specifically assigned to the service of the Loan.

6. The Secretary of the Treasury failed to prepare and submit to the Financial Adviser the budget at the time and in the manner as specifically required by the Loan Agreement, although the Government had been previously notified by the Financial Adviser of the time provided for such preparation and submission, thus delaying and hampering the administration of the Fiscal Service of the Loan.

7. The Liberian Government has denied the authority of nomination of an acting Financial Adviser by the President of the United States under the Loan Agreement.

8. Upon remonstrance by American Supervisor of Customs against unlawful shipment of certain labor from Montserrado, the Secretary of the Treasury replied in writing approving and directing such action asserting that 'the organic law of this country . . . gives the President the right to set aside or annul any existing acts of the Legislature. No subordinate administrative official in the President's administration can refuse to comply with his instructions, and when this is done he becomes personally responsible and answerable.'

9. The authority of the Financial Adviser over the officers of the Fiscal Service has been repeatedly and openly challenged and a program of obstruction to the service of the Loan has been carried out by the Liberian Government; for example:

a. In derogation of the express terms and intent of the Loan Agreement, the Government addressed the Financial Adviser in writing, asserting that the Financial Adviser is a member of and subject to the Treasury Department of the Government of Liberia.

b. In derogation of the express terms and intent of the Loan Agreement, the Government addressed a communication from its Solicitor General to the Financial Adviser, asserting that the Supervisor of Internal Revenue is a member of the Treasury Department of Liberia and is subject to the Secretary of the Treasury.

c. From time to time the Government has appointed to the Customs and Internal Revenue Service officials and employees without the previous advice of the Financial Adviser as contemplated in Article IX; and without previous consultation with or the information to the Financial Adviser.

d. The Attorney General has continually opposed and repeatedly failed to comply with Executive Order No. 3, in so far as it relates to the control of purchases of food for prisoners, though officially his attention has been called to his omission to comply with the said Executive Order.

e. The salary of one of the foreign Consuls has been increased without notice to, consultation with or approval of the Liberian Legislature or the Financial Adviser.

f. The Secretary of the Interior while also Acting Secretary of the Treasury, after a payroll had been audited by the Auditor and warrant for such payroll had been signed, mutilated and altered such payroll by crossing out thereon the name of a Department of Interior employee named Labor, and substituted therefor the name of another individual.

g. Following protest by the Financial Adviser to the Government against such unlawful act, the Government subsequently appointed such Acting Secretary of the Treasury to the position of Secretary of the Treasury which he now continues to hold.

h. The Secretary of the Treasury stated to a claimant against the Government, prior to a hearing on such claim before the Claims Commission of which the Secretary of the Treasury was a member, that he was in favor of and would vote for such claim but that he was unable to state what action the Financial

Adviser and the American Auditor, the other members of the Claims Commission, would take upon such claim.

i. Despite proof of repeated acts of obstruction to the service of the Loan made by Financial Adviser to the Government against the Secretary of the Treasury in the presence of such Secretary of the Treasury, of the American Auditor and of the American Supervisor of Customs, and request for relief therefrom, the conduct of interference and obstruction by the Secretary of the Treasury in such regard continues.

j. Government officials have failed for more than a year to accept or act upon suggestions of the Financial Adviser that income of the Government was diminishing to the point that it would be insufficient to meet the budget and that steps to reduce expenses should be immediately taken and measures to provide additional revenues should be adopted, which omission to promptly act upon such suggestions has threatened impairment of the security of the Loan.

These instances have compelled us to reach the conclusion hereinbefore stated.

We acknowledge receipt of your letter of May 16, 1930 transmitting to us a copy of the request of the Financial Adviser to be advised if funds will be available from delivery of Liberian bonds as requested. A copy of this communication will suffice we feel sure as an answer to the inquiry of the Financial Adviser.

We likewise acknowledge receipt of your letter of May 22, 1930 enclosing a copy of a communication to you from the Secretary of the Treasury of Liberia, dated May 3, 1930 (with memorandum attached dated April 23, 1930) soliciting your good offices to assist the Government of Liberia in consummating with the Bank of British West Africa a loan of funds for the purpose of meeting the deficit which the Secretary advises exists between revenues available and expenditures necessary to meet the Budget for the calendar year 1930, and claiming authority on the part of the Government to conclude such an arrangement under Article XV of the Loan Agreement.

There is no anticipated revenue available to the Government of Liberia for the remainder of this fiscal year sufficient to meet the present Budget and liquidate this suggested loan, and there-

fore Article XV contains no sanction for making such a loan
without the approval of the Financial Adviser which is withheld, in our opinion for good cause because it seems to us that
in the best interest of all parties to the Loan Agreement no
expedient should be adopted which would hypothecate the revenues of the Government already pledged to the security of the
Loan.

In response to the request of the Secretary of the Treasury
that we suggest some other way of bringing about relief of the
present situation, we respectfully submit the following recommendation:

The 1925 budget of the Liberian Government provided
$263,229.20 to cover the cost of those functions of the Govern-
ment which the 1930 budget provides, shall be paid from unassigned revenues. We believe if on July 1, 1930 the Government
would reduce its budget to a basis of $325,000 for annual ex-
penditures out of unassigned revenues, instead of approximately
$450,000 as the 1930 budget now provides and, in addition,
would defer approximately $100,000 of current accounts paya-
ble from unassigned revenues for payment out of the next annual budget, that this would be an effective way for the Liberian Government to accomplish its purpose.

Finance Corporation is certain, now that the above facts have
been brought to the attention of the Liberian Government,
that the Government will promptly remedy the conditions set
out above with respect to the administration of the Loan
Agreement and in this belief Finance Corporation is quite willing, in order to avoid embarrassment to the Liberian Government meanwhile, and without prejudice to its rights and its
position as outlined above, to take up $18,000 face value of
bonds immediately for the following specific purposes provided
in the 1930 budget as follows:

$11,000 being the difference between the $18,000 for special
sanitation work appropriated in the budget and
$7,000 furnished from other sources for this pur-
pose.

5,000 for the grant of aid to the Booker T. Washington
Agricultural and Industrial Institute.

We request that a copy of this communication be transmitted by you to the Liberian Government and to the Financial Adviser and we are filing a copy thereof with the Department of State of the United States.

Respectfully submitted,

FINANCE CORPORATION OF AMERICA."

ENCLOSURE THREE.

COPY OF LETTER DATED OCTOBER 1, 1930, FROM PRESIDENT KING, IN REPLY TO LETTER DATED JUNE 14, 1930, FROM THE FINANCE CORPORATION OF AMERICA.

"EXECUTIVE MANSION,
Monrovia, Liberia, October 1, 1930.

THE NATIONAL CITY BANK OF NEW YORK,
Fiscal Agents of Loan Agreement of 1926,
New York, U. S. A.

SIRS:

In reply to Finance Corporation's communication dated June 14, 1930, addressed to the Fiscal Agents of the Loan Agreement of September 1, 1926, please be informed that this letter has been given careful consideration.

The Liberian Government consider it unnecessary to submit the alleged breaches of the Loan Agreement to arbitration. It is thought that the divergent views of the Liberian Government and Finance Corporation may be reconciled otherwise. I take occasion therefore to express frankly the views of the Liberian Government in the hope that the breaches complained of may be corrected.

1. The Liberian Government assures Finance Corporation that it will not question the disbursement of assigned revenues in the order stated in Article 13, page 20 and 21 of the Loan Agreement; neither will the Secretary of the Treasury withhold the application of assigned revenues to the liquidation of accounts legally approved by the Financial Adviser as due and payable from such funds.

2. The Liberian Government disavows intention of denying the Financial Adviser the authority given him to make rules and regulations governing the operation of fiscal matters in

accordance with Article 12 of the Loan Agreement. The Government is of the opinion, however, that Executive Order No. 9, upon which charge of breach is based, should be rewritten to provide that prior to the issuance of Transfer Order from Government general accounts to the disbursement account, an Executive Warrant shall be approved. This is in accord with a Constitutional provision. The Financial Adviser has been directed to draft, for Executive approval, a new Order observing the constitutional provision, as well as providing for the insertion of serial check numbers on the Transfer Order.

3. The Liberian Government has not yet designated an official Depositary because of difference in opinion growing out of an attempt to execute a depositary contract with the Bank of British West Africa. This subject will again be taken up when banking facilities are available in Monrovia.

4. The allegation that the Secretary of State and the Secretary of the Treasury have failed to compel certain consular officers to submit accounting of pay and salary fees into the Treasury is having the immediate consideration of the Government. The Government is anxious that public revenues from every source shall be deposited into the Treasury in accordance with the laws and lawful regulations of the Republic. Finance Corporation is assured that the Government will take steps to bring to account the revenues arising from consular receipts. Towards this end the Financial Adviser has been requested to prepare appropriate regulations.

5. The charge contained in paragraph 5 of Finance Corporation's letter has been a matter of serious concern to the Head of the Government of Liberia.

It should be borne in mind that the President of Liberia is without authority to control findings of juries. The action of one juror may defeat the ends of justice. The cases which Finance Corporation must have in mind were not handled to the satisfaction of the President of Liberia. Measures for effecting the forfeiture of bonds of public officials who fail to account for public revenues received by them will be worked out. Directions have been given to the Financial Adviser to study existing laws with a view to drafting such legislation as will authorize the setting up of a Bond Commission or Administrative Court which will be charged with the duty of determining, without the aid of a jury, when the bond of a defaulting official and or his sureties shall be escheated. The finding of this court shall be final and conclusive of the matter, saving, however, the right of the defendant to appeal to the Supreme Court.

6. The complaint touching the failure of the Secretary of the Treasury to submit to the Financial Adviser the Budget at the time and in the manner specifically required by the Loan Agreement, may again arise because the time within which corrective measures could be adopted this year has passed. Finance Corporation is assured that steps will be taken to readjust the administration of the Treasury.

7. The Liberian Government hold a different view of the matter complained of in paragraph 7, namely, the nomination of the Acting Financial Adviser. The view of the Liberian Government is that the Financial Adviser does not lose his status while absent on leave. The Liberian Government has held to the opinion that notwithstanding the absence of the Financial Adviser from his post of duty he cannot divest himself of the responsibility for the proper performance and carrying on of the business of the office. To make it possible for the Financial Adviser to control his office in his absence, and to hold him responsible, he himself should select the official who acts in his stead. This is a procedure calculated to secure continuity of policy in an important office.

8. The statement made by the Secretary of the Treasury to the effect that under the organic law of Liberia the President has the right to set aside or annul any existing acts of the Legislature, is unauthorized and not warranted under either the organic or Statutory laws of the Republic.

9. The basis of the authority of the Financial Adviser is fixed in the Loan Agreement and the Government will support his authority expressly granted or that which may be lawfully implied.

Under Article 9 of the Loan Agreement the status of Fiscal Officers is specifically fixed and these officers, in the performance of their duties, are responsible to the Financial Adviser.

(i) The matter complained of in paragraph 8 of Finance Corporation's letter will be remedied by administrative action.

(1) The Liberian Government is agreeable to the Financial Adviser making suggestions and offering plans to rehabilitate the

finances of the Government and to his preparing regulations for financial administration. Finance Corporation may be certain that the Liberian Government will give appropriate attention to suggestions of the Financial Adviser which are not contrary to the constitution and laws of Liberia. It is believed that the corrective measures set out in this letter together with the assurance of coöperation will satisfy all concerned as to the Liberian Government's intention to adjust apparent differences of opinion and settle questions which have arisen concerning procedure.

Yours very truly,

(signed) C. D. B. KING,
President of Liberia."

ENCLOSURE FOUR.

LIST OF THIRTY-ONE RECOMMENDATIONS MADE TO THE LI-
BERIAN GOVERNMENT BY THE FINANCIAL ADVISER, BETWEEN
1929 AND 1932.

Date	Subject	Action taken
June 8, 1929...	Recommending that Consular officers be requested to deposit Consular fees.	None
June 18, 1929..	Special report to the President detailing recommendations for economies in connection with all Departments.	No action taken during the ensuing six months of 1929. Subsequently some of the economies suggested were effected.
Sept. 18, 1929..	Reduce Government personnel, reduce budget, reduce Frontier Force.	None
Jan. 17, 1930...	Complete Monrovia Customs House.	None
April 7, 1930...	Necessity of materially reducing expenses.	None
Aug. 6, 1930...	Recommending law providing penalty for delinquent taxpayers in order to improve collections.	None
Aug. 13, 1930..	Recommending geological survey.	None
Sept. 30, 1930..	Construct roads to develop hinterland trade so that exports now crossing Liberian hinterland boundaries would be sent to Liberian ports.	None
Sept. 30, 1930..	Open hinterland to foreign traders by removal of all restrictions.	(A similar recommendation was made in the Report of the International Commission submitted to the Liberian Government on September 8, 1930. A Law was passed on this subject in December 1930. So

List of Thirty-one Recommendations Made to the Liberian Government by the Financial Adviser, Between
1929 and 1932.—Continued.

Date	Subject	Action taken
Sept. 30, 1930..		far as is known no foreign trader has established himself subsequently in the hinterland. There is one foreign trading firm at Kakata fifty miles from Monrovia).
Sept. 30, 1930..	Provide for the continuous maintenance of the roads already constructed.	Practically no maintenance work is done on roads. (For example a bridge on the Monrovia-Kakata road which collapsed in April 1933, cutting off all traffic to Kakata, was not repaired for over four weeks.)
Sept. 30, 1930..	Improve Judiciary, simplify procedure, provide commercial code.	None
Sept. 30, 1930..	Close or lease Government radio station.	None
Sept. 30, 1930..	Recommendation that Consuls be forced to deposit their fees, their failure to do so constituting a violation of the Liberian Constitution as well as of the Loan Agreement and the existing Consular Regulations.	None
June 18, 1931..	County Supts. to act as District Commissioners or vice versa in the interest of economy.	None
June 23, 1931..	Secretary of War to act as Commander of Frontier Force or vice versa in the interest of economy.	None

LIST OF THIRTY-ONE RECOMMENDATIONS MADE TO THE LI-
BERIAN GOVERNMENT BY THE FINANCIAL ADVISER, BETWEEN
1929 AND 1932.—Continued.

Date	Subject	Action taken
June 23, 1931..	Government radio station to be closed or leased.	None
June 23, 1931..	Secretary of the Treasury to reduce the number of buildings rented for Government purposes.	None
June 23, 1931..	Reduction of Government staffs in the various departments and increase of office hours by one hour.	None
June 23, 1931..	Recommendation that Customs defaulters and officials short in cash accounts should be prosecuted; recommendation that the Government act on bonds of delinquent officials.	None
Oct. 13, 1931...	Extend Monrovia-Kakata road in the hinterland; develop hinterland and encourage traders to extend their activities.	None
Nov. 24, 1931..	Deposit of court costs and fees; pay expenses from budget appropriation.	None
Nov. 24, 1931..	To insure receipt of funds by Government, have Consular fees on imports collected by the Bureau of Customs; Consuls to be paid from budget appropriation.	None
April 29, 1931..	The floating debt should not be permitted to increase.	The floating debt continued to increase.
April 29, 1931..	Combine the duties of the Secretary of War and the Commander of the Frontier Force; the Secretary of Public Instruction and the Secretary of the Interior; Postmaster General	None

List of Thirty-one Recommendations Made to the Liberian Government by the Financial Adviser, Between 1929 and 1932.—Continued.

Date	Subject	Action taken
April 29, 1931..	and the Secretary of the Treasury.	
April 29, 1932..	Close or lease Government radio station.	None
April 29, 1932..	Reduce personnel of Departments.	None on record except in the administration of the Financial Adviser.
Sept. 23, 1932..	Close or lease Government radio station.	None
Sept. 23, 1932..	Systematic plan for the upkeep of existing roads.	None: (See comment in connection with recommendation dated Sept. 30, 1930)
Sept. 23, 1932..	Recommendations for enforcing the deposit of Consular fees due to the Government.	None
Sept. 23, 1932..	Necessity to curtail increase in floating debt.	None
Sept. 23, 1932..	Failure of the Government to prosecute violators of the revenue laws.	None

ENCLOSURE FIVE.

List of Fifteen Recent Incorrect Statements Made by Secretary of State Grimes, Together with the Pertinent Corrections.

1. Mr. Grimes states (pages 18–19) with reference to the budget of 1928–29 that after a "sudden unexpected decline in revenues from all sources became apparent" the Government acted "promptly upon the advice of the Financial Adviser," effecting a cut in expenses which nevertheless proved insufficient to meet the situation, leaving unpaid obligations of about $148,-000 at the end of the fiscal year.

Mr. Grimes' statement that expenses were cut by $151,000 should be qualified by an explanation that only approximately one-half of this cut was in expenses payable from revenues, the balance being a reduction in proposed expenditures from Loan funds. At the time the cut was made the Financial Adviser recommended further economies, and later in the year their necessity was again emphasised. Had the advice of the Financial Adviser been followed the fiscal year would have closed without the deficit of approximately $148,000 referred to. Had the budget been reduced fully as recommended by the Financial Adviser it would still have been approximately the same as the budget for the previous year (1927–28) which was $1,126,000.

2. Mr. Grimes states (page 19) that the budget for 1929–30 authorised expenditures of $1,028,000 which included provision for paying the deficit of $148,000 from the previous year and left $880,000 for the expenses of the Government for the year 1929–30, distributed as follows:

(a) Priority payments under the Loan Agreement
   payable from assigned revenues:
   Salaries $157,556.92
   Loan charges 210,437.50
   Other expenses 80,647.60

   making a total of $448,642.02
(b) Ordinary expenses, payable from unassigned
   revenues and any residue of assigned revenues:
   Salaries $346,036.40
   Other charges 85,328.79

   making a total of..................... $431,365.19

Mr. Grimes' object in submitting the above tables was apparently to try to prove that the $880,000 for the operating expenses of the Liberian Government, over 50% were required to meet charges arising from the Loan. However, Mr. Grimes has included in the priority payments which he infers resulted from the Loan, the cost of maintaining the Frontier Force, and the entire cost of the bureaux of Customs, Internal Revenue and

Audits, which services would be maintained regardless of the Loan. To give an accurate picture, the following table should be substituted for table (a) above:

Salaries of Fiscal Officers..................... $37,000.00
Interest on the Loan.......................... 175,000.00
Other expenses (allowances Fiscal Agent, Finan-
    cial Adviser's staff) 15,198.14

These three items total $227,198.14, or approximately 20% of $880,000, instead of a total of over $448,000 or over 50% of $880,000, as given by Mr. Grimes. This inaccuracy in Mr. Grimes' figures was made a matter of official record by the Financial Adviser shortly after Mr. Grimes first publicly made this allegation during the previous year. The correct figures give a balance available during that year for the ordinary expenses of the Liberian Government (not connected with the Loan or the previous year's deficit) of approximately $650,000 instead of approximately $430,000 as alleged by Mr. Grimes.

3. Mr. Grimes refers (middle of page 20) to a "difference of $159,660.42 between appropriations and available funds" representing outstanding obligations chargeable to unassigned revenues.

Mr. Grimes failed to state that the deficit of $148,000 outstanding on December 31, 1929, was included in the above $159,660.42.

4. Mr. Grimes states (page 21) that certain measures suggested by the Financial Adviser "were not adequate to relieve the situation."

The measures suggested by the Financial Adviser were adequate to prevent a further increase in indebtedness and would in fact have resulted in a decrease. In any case the suggestions were not carried out by the Liberian Government.

5. In regard to Mr. Grimes' allegations appearing on pages 23 to 25, in connection with efforts on the part of the Government to obtain further advances from the Finance Corporation, reference is made to the reply of the Finance Corporation dated June 14, 1930. The Liberian Government admitted the correctness of the majority of the complaints in its acknowledgment of October 1, 1930. (The full texts appear as Enclosures three and four.)

6. Mr. Grimes states (bottom page 25) that a "minority report, submitted by the Financial Adviser" recommended the reduction of expenditures in the personnel and pay of every department of the Government "save and except the Bureaux and services operating under the Loan."

Under item 6 of his "minority report" the Financial Adviser specifically recommended reductions in the Bureau of Customs. This Bureau was cut from $159,000 in 1928 to $65,000 in 1930, and to $45,000 in 1932. The Bureaux of Audit and of Internal Revenue were at the time under-staffed and the office of the Financial Adviser himself consisted of one chief clerk, one clerk (who was detailed to one of the Revenue collecting Bureaux) and one messenger. The Financial Adviser's budget (excluding his salary) was reduced from $8,320 in 1930 to $2,637 in 1932.

7. Mr. Grimes refers (page 27) to a memorandum forwarded to the Finance Corporation in September 1931, containing assurances of economies to be put into effect by the Liberian Government and expressing the hope that the Government would be able to pay the interest and amortisation due on November 1, 1931, before the end of that year.

These promised economies were not put into effect by the Liberian Government, nor was the interest paid by the end of 1931.

8. Mr. Grimes further states (page 27) that "as a mark of good faith the Government engaged to earmark *all hut and other taxes*" until interest and amortisation charges had been met.

The Liberian Government engaged to earmark *only hut and real estate taxes*. The hut tax is paid by the natives. The real estate tax, nearly all of which is due from Americo-Liberians, amounts to only approximately $4,000 per year, of which over 80% is delinquent each year, the arrears never being collected because of the failure to prosecute on the part of the Department of Justice. This situation has been brought to the attention of the Liberian Government by the Financial Adviser on repeated occasions.

9. Mr. Grimes states (page 28) that "the continuous efflux" of large sums of money required for the payment of interest and amortisation "constituted a steady drain outward of the money available for circulation."

The amounts transferred abroad by Liberia on account of interest and amortisation have been far more than compensated for by the funds imported into Liberia to pay Firestone operating expenses, and by the donations by the missions and philanthropic organisations for their work in Liberia. Liberia's visible imports have consistently exceeded the visible exports ever since the Loan became effective in 1927. In one year the surplus of visible imports was $2,500,000 and in 1931 it was $179,000. Thus there must have been a large continuing influx of money into Liberia, and not an efflux.[38]

10. Mr. Grimes states (page 28) that by May 1932 "conditions had reached a point that employees of the Government, not serving under the Loan Agreement, could no longer be expected to continue to evince that loyalty to the public service as has characterised their conduct in the past by remaining daily at their posts of duty without being paid." Mr. Grimes attempts in this and other reports and complaints to show that Liberia's personnel had not been paid; that the majority of employees had been working faithfully without compensation; and that the revenues were largely used for Loan service.

Of the total of 1090 Liberian officials, employees and native officials in 1932, 754 were paid their full salaries regularly month by month up to and including November 1932 (the last month prior to the unilateral violation of the Loan Agreement

[38]Mr. Grimes makes a somewhat similar allegation in item 10 of his memorandum submitted following the adoption by the International Committee on June 27, 1933 of the revised League Plan (League Document C.421.M.214, p. 3) when he states that "to pay such huge salaries as those contemplated in the report to foreign officials and such parsimonious salaries to the Liberian officials and employees will disturb the balance of circulation of money and cause a steady drain of money out of the country that will ultimately increase rather than relieve the present distress."

In a memorandum read to the International Committee at its meeting of June 23 Mr. Grimes also referred to the "amounts paid to persons of foreign nationality" and complained that they "exported most of the money for their salaries . . . and lived in Liberia principally on their allowances." After six years as a Liberian official during the operation of the Loan Contract, Mr. Grimes could hardly have been unaware of the fact that although the foreign fiscal officials receive their quarters and medical attention from the Liberian Government, they receive *no cash allowances whatever.*

by the Liberian Government); and the 29 employees of the
Legislature (not members) were also paid in full. The remaining 317 officials and employees were paid irregularly but
on the whole received substantial sums some of which were as
follows:

The President $10,983.33
Secretary of State Grimes 7,629.40
The Vice-President 2,077.50
The Secretary of the Treasury............... 3,137.98

As enclosure six a complete list of these 317 Liberian officials
and employees is furnished showing that out of approximately
$137,000 from unassigned revenue during 1932, over $118,000
was paid to Liberians *not connected in any manner with the
services of the Loan.*

11. Mr. Grimes summarises (pages 29–30) a set of proposals
made by the Liberian Government to the Finance Corporation
of America on September 23rd, 1932, and states that assurances
were given the Corporation by the Liberian Government of a
"rigid economy" to balance the budget for 1933. He also states
that a copy of the proposed budget for 1933 was sent to the
Corporation at the same time and infers that the Acting Financial Adviser, who delivered the above documents to the Finance
Corporation, endorsed the proposals.

The Liberian unilateral actions taken on December 17th,
1932, and thereafter did not correspond to the Liberian proposals made to the Finance Corporation by letter of September 23rd. The proposed budget for 1933 forwarded on September 23rd, 1932, is not the one under which Liberia has been
operating in 1933, numerous items of expenses not mentioned
in connection with the first budget being included in the illegal
budget now in use, while items required by law to be included
have not been provided for. Mr. McCaskey[89] did not undertake
to obtain consent of the Finance Corporation to the modifications proposed on September 23rd, 1932, but merely acted as
transmitting agent.

The 1933 Liberian budget was not passed by the Liberian
Legislature until the end of January 1933. Since the represen-

[89]Prior to his service in Liberia, Mr. McCaskey had served as
Treasurer and Director-General of the Budget of Persia.

tative of the Finance Corporation reached Monrovia on December 11th, 1932, with his company's replies to the Liberian proposals of September 23rd, 1932, there was ample time for a legal budget for 1933 to have been considered by the Liberian Government.

12. Mr. Grimes states (page 31) that "the salaries of the entire Liberian personnel of the civil establishment had been twice reduced, once as much as 50%; with the result that none of said officials, from the highest to the lowest, was receiving a living wage."

Only a very few of the Liberian personnel suffered a reduction of 50% much of the "economy" having been effected by a reduction in the number of personnel. Furthermore, present budgetary allowances for Liberian personnel are approximately the same as they were in 1924, before the negotiation of either the Loan Agreement or the Firestone Plantation Contract. A reference to the annexed list (Enclosure 6) indicates that during 1932 large sums were received by the highest Liberian officials (including Mr. Grimes). Many of the Liberian officials and employees received their full salaries.

13. Mr. Grimes discusses (page 35) the state of the Liberian public debt.

Mr. Grimes fails to state that the creation of the floating debt was unlawful, and that if the repeated advice of the Financial Adviser had been followed there would have been no floating debt.

It is absurd to deplore the smallness of Liberian revenues. Had the advice repeatedly given by the fiscal officers been followed, Liberian revenues would have been very much greater. Revenue returns from neighbouring countries in 1930 are quoted below to indicate the possibilities of Liberia:

Country	Area	Revenues
Liberia	43,000 square miles	$840,472.00
Dahomey	41,302 " "	2,220,000.00
Sierra Leone	31,000 " "	3,211,137.00
French Togoland	20,000 " "	2,074,760.00
Portuguese Guinea	14,100 " "	704,545.00
British Gambia	4,134 " "	1,040,000.00

(From African Handbook for 1930).

38449

Liberia will show increased revenues, sufficient to meet all legitimate expenses, when expert economic advice is accepted and honestly followed. In this connection, commenting on the situation in 1931 in their official report the League Experts state:

"Liberia needs expert advisers, and will need them for many years to come. These advisers should not only give advice, which would not be sufficient, *but should have actual authority*." (League Document No. C.469.M.238, p. 33).[40]

14. Mr. Grimes states (page 35) that there was "no intention on the part of the Government of Liberia to modify unilaterally, as has been alleged by the American member of the Committee, the contract existing between the said Government and the Finance Corporation of America." In support of this statement, Mr. Grimes quotes the last two sections only of the legislation in question. This Act (of December 23, 1932) in previous sections, which Mr. Grimes omits, not only suspends interest and amortization payments, reduces the salaries of Fiscal Officers, and reduces their number, but it also seeks to void the clause in the Loan Agreement relative to assigned revenues and

---

[40]The experiences of the Public Health Adviser to Liberia have already been mentioned. References should also be made to the Adviser to the Liberian Frontier Force appointed under the Loan Agreement.

Col. George Lewis was formerly in the Porto Rican Constabulary, an organization of 1,100 officers and men. He was appointed Adviser to the Frontier Force and reached Monrovia on June 14, 1930. The Liberian Government commissioned Col. Lewis a "Major" in the Frontier Force, an organization of approximately 500 officers and men. He was given inadequate quarters in the "War Department" and instructed to prepare drill regulations.

Serious difficulties developed on the Kru Coast in the early summer of 1931 and the need of experience in meeting the situation soon became abundantly evident. Although a detachment of the Frontier Force was sent to the Kru Coast, the Liberian Government neither solicited Col. Lewis' advice nor made use of his services in any way in connection with the expedition. The history of the subsequent "pacification of the natives" is sufficiently well-known. It led to formal protests by the British, French and American Governments.

Col. Lewis left Monrovia on December 24, 1931, and shortly thereafter resigned.

priority payments. It seriously impairs if not destroys, the guarantees and securities of the Loan.[41]

Mr. Grimes made the statement quoted above on February 7th, 1933. The American Representative on the International Committee has a list of over thirty acts by the Liberian Government in violation of the Loan Agreement of 1926. This list covers the period from December 15th, 1932, to March 10th, 1933, only.

15. Finally, Mr. Grimes informed the International Committee on Liberia at a meeting in June 1933 that Liberian revenues had increased since the Government had taken exclusive charge of collections.

The Fiscal Officials under the Loan Agreement have not been permitted to function since the beginning of 1933. Liberian revenues for the first six months of 1932 were $265,419.99; for the first six months of 1933 they were $216,021.28, *a decrease* of $49,398.71.

[41] On pages 1410–1411 of the League Official Journal the following statement appears, made by the Liberian representative:

"During the life of the present Loan Agreement, existing statutes and regulations governing the collection of Customs and excise will remain in force, and the foreign fiscal officers agreed upon to function thereunder will be retained, subject to any arrangements which, as contemplated under proposal three, may be made direct with the Finance Corporation of America . . . The foreign fiscal officers, functioning under the present Loan Agreement will remain in the service of the Republic unless arrangements for reducing their number can be made directly between the contracting parties with such moral support as the League of Nations may give."

ENCLOSURE SIX

COMPLETE LIST OF 317 LIBERIAN OFFICIALS AND EMPLOYEES, SHOWING THE AMOUNTS RECEIVED BY EACH DURING 1932.

(Reference: Enclosure Five, Item 10 of the corrections of statements made by Secretary of State Grimes).

REPUBLIC OF LIBERIA.

Payments from unassigned revenues, January 1, 1932, to December 31, 1932 inclusive, listed alphabetically by names of payees.

Name	Amount	Name	Amount
Ash, I. T............	$25.00	Brown, John A.....	$116.66
		Brown, John W.....	100.00
Bailey, C. B........	40.00	Brumskine, W. P. L.	91.66
Barclay, Arthur......	1,074.16	Bryant, C. M.......	533.32
Barclay, Edwin......	10,983.33	Bryant, W. A.......	351.11
Barnes, N. H.......	75.00	Bryant, William....	40.00
Bassil, J. K. P......	623.32	Bryant, W. H.......	187.50
Benson, J. A........	46.66	Buchanan, Thos. E..	600.00
Bedell, R. L........	174.99	Bull, F. J..........	67.75
Berrian, C. T.......	22.50	Bull, J. E..........	165.00
Berry, Susan........	37.50	Burke, Charlie......	22.50
Beysolow, T. E......	1,241.66		
Biondi, Antonio......	4,271.60	Cain, G. B.........	161.40
Birch, H. C.........	225.00	Cain, Monroe.......	40.00
Bishop, A. T........	25.00	Capehart, R. A. T...	22.50
Blake, W. T........	100.00	Cassell, C. A.......	33.60
Boyce, J. A.........	40.00	Cassell, N. H. B.....	433.32
Bracewell, Johnny....	25.00	Cavalla River Co...	450.98
Brandy, William.....	25.00	Cephas, D. L.......	48.00
Boyle, W. S.........	50.00	Chesson, J. J.......	22.50
Brewer, G. T., Sr.....	272.00	Campbell, C. R.....	375.00
Brewer, R. A........	480.00	Clarke, Jacob......	40.00
Briggs, Stephen......	40.00	Clarke, J. R........	58.33
Bright, R. E........	25.00	Clarke, W. J.......	623.32
Bright, W. O. D., Sr..	166.66	Cleon, W. H.......	50.00
Bright, W. O. D., Jr..	59.76	Clinton, A. B......	87.49
Brown, D. B........	750.00	Chenoweth, C. H....	191.66
Brown, Chancy......	40.00	Chiles, Ezekiel......	22.50
Brown, Jacob........	83.32	Cole, J. A.........	375.00
Brown, V. F........	22.50	Coleman, S. D......	533.32

Payments from unassigned revenues, January 1, 1932, to December 31, 1932 inclusive, listed alphabetically by names of payees.—Continued.

Name	Amount	Name	Amount
Coleman, Charles S..	$100.00	Dobson, J. D.	$25.00
Coleman, J. E.	125.00	Dounoum, J. L.	183.32
Coleman, J. F. B.	112.50	Dossen, J. A.	41.66
Collins, B. T.	300.00	Dossen, S. J.	677.32
Cooper, J. R.	99.99	Dunn, Edward	233.32
Cooper, Johnny	21.25	Dunbar, G. A.	141.66
Cooper, J. F.	300.24	Dunbar, J. F.	1,274.20
Cooper, H. J. R.	124.98	Dunbar, Tillman.	37.50
Cooper, H. R. F.	43.50	Duncan, H. B.	388.33
Cooper, H. R.	394.98	Dyson, J. B.	50.00
Cooper, R. F. R.	300.00		
Crayton, J. R.	75.00	Eastman, J.	40.00
Crump, Samuel B.	40.00	Eastman, T. E.	125.00
Cummins, Moses.	21.58	Elder Dempster.	36.00
Cummings, J. T.	133.32	Ellis, R. L.	50.00
		Elias Bros.	79.38
David, I. A.	100.00	Ethridge, Edward.	22.50
Davis, F. H.	50.00		
Davis, J. L.	50.00	Faabule, E. O.	205.00
Davies, T. E.	612.66	Fahnbulleh, J.	58.33
Dayrell, J. T., Sr.	150.00	Ferguson, M. Z.	114.58
Dayrell, Mary A. P..	40.00	Ficklin, Andrew.	22.50
Dayrell, J. T., Jr.	150.00	Firestone Plantations	8,490.37
Dennis, C. G.	96.00	Flowers, P. L.	40.00
Dennis, J. F.	375.00	Freeman, Annie.	267.33
Dennis, J. B.	150.00	Freeman, D. D.	22.50
Dennis, John.	22.50	Freeman, W. H.	21.25
Dennis, J. Samuel.	625.00	Freeman and Ricks..	50.00
Dennis, J. W.	223.46	French Company.	1,519.06
Dennis, J. E.	75.00	Fredericks, Harold..	395.42
Dennis, Maria.	187.50	Frey and Zusli.	398.46
Dennis, Charles H.	165.00	Fuszek, R. G.	9,625.72
Dennis, M. L.	180.00		
Dennis, G. L.	3,137.97	Gabbidon, Samuel A.	99.99
De Sola Bors.	387.30	Garnett, E. S.	108.33
Dickerson, S. H.	700.00	Gemayel Bros.	250.08
Diggs, M. T.	75.00	George, A. J.	700.00
Dinklage, M.	115.20	George and Son, A. J.	405.91
Dixon, R. E.	600.00	Gibson, C.	20.83
Diggs, A. T.	25.00	Gibson, J. E.	91.66
Diggs, J. T.	273.00	Gibson, G. W.	603.80
Dingwall, J. A.	1,008.27	Gibson, N. H.	141.66

Payments from unassigned revenues, January 1, 1932, to December 31, 1932 inclusive, listed alphabetically by names of payees.—Continued.

Name	Amount	Name	Amount
Gibson, J. C. A., Jr...	$129.69	Jones, J. D.........	$158.32
Gittens, James A.....	48.00	Jones, H. E.........	25.00
Gittens, L. R........	154.15	Jones, J. E.........	550.00
Gofiah, Isaac........	25.00	Jones, J. A. H......	605.32
Goodlan, J. W.......	22.50	Johnny............	24.00
Gordon, J. T........	41.66	Johns, T. W........	50.00
Gordon, R. W........	605.32	Johns, J. C.........	156.00
Grisby, Samuel J.....	1,241.66	Johnson, H. W......	75.00
Greaves, W. R.......	46.66	Johnson, F. E. R....	1,408.35
Grimes, Frank T.....	100.00	Johnson, G. G.....	116.66
Grimes, Henry......	100.00	Johnson, Jas. E.....	41.66
Grimes, L A........	7,629.40	Johnson, G. M......	496.00
		Johnson, Gray S....	25.00
Harmon, Emmett....	60.00	Johnson, C. W. D...	313.33
Harmon, Joseph P.,.		Johnson, Jeriette....	233.32
Jr...............	191.66	Johnson, Carney....	33.33
Harmon, S. J. L......	62.50	Johnson, Thomas...	41.66
Harris, P. T.........	22.50		
Harris, J. J..........	375.00	Karnga, A. W......	1,241.66
Hayes, H. G........	360.00	King, C. D. B......	41.66
Hayes, L. M.........	22.50	King, Caesar.......	25.00
Hayes, W. H........	25.00	King, C. H. W.....	100.00
Henry, C. H........	50.00	Klingie, J. G.......	100.00
Henries, R. A.......	233.30	Knuckles, Mary E...	41.66
Hill, Hannah........	48.00		
Hilton, M. E. M....	166.66	Lawrence, J. D.....	50.00
Holder, J. B........	25.00	Lawrence, Rosetta..	40.00
Holder, R. N.......	533.32	Liberia College.....	528.00
Holland, F. H. and		Liberty, H. J. E.....	67.50
Co.	499.42	L. F. F. Old Soldiers	2,001.66
Horrace, J. B........	605.32	Luke, Henry E.....	50.00
Horrace, S. R........	174.99		
Howard, D. E.......	250.00	Majors, C. D.......	623.32
Howard, D. M......	208.30	Mars, A. B.........	22.50
Howard, J. Y........	405.00	Marshall, I. W.....	200.00
Howard, P. F.......	174.99	Marshall, J. F......	200.00
Howard, Phillip.....	41.66	Marshall, J. T......	41.66
		Marshall, T. G.....	20.83
Innis, J. T..........	41.66	Massaquoi, M. E....	100.00
		Massaquoi, M.......	330.00
Jackson, William....	22.00	Maxmore, J. H. F...	25.00
Jones, Elfrieda E.....	75.00	McBorrough, W. J..	54.00

Payments from unassigned revenues, January 1, 1932, to December 31, 1932 inclusive, listed alphabetically by names of payees.—Continued.

Name	Amount	Name	Amount
McClain, J. W. H....	$666.66	Pearson, H. F......	$20.00
McCauley, D. B......	39.64	Pearson, J. W.......	272.00
McCritty, James B...	100.00	Phillips, Hilary.....	25.00
McWillie, Herman...	150.00	Pitman, Louis......	280.00
Melton, J. S........	22.50	Pritchard, Wallace..	40.00
Mends-Cole, J. A.....	112.50	Potter, U. A........	605.32
Minor, C. A. (heirs)..	250.00	Potter, J. D........	40.00
Minor, Jas. J.	493.55	P. Z. & Company...	421.41
Milton, N. T........	50.00		
Mitchell, J. S........	133.32	Quah, Alfred......	24.00
Monger, A. C........	133.32		
Monger, E. A........	75.86	Radio Corp. of	
Montgomery, R. S....	56.25	America........	232.56
Moore, John M.....	133.34	Railey, James A.....	54.16
Moore, June........	360.00	Railey, Wm........	25.00
Moore, Laura A.....	40.00	Reeves, Jude F.... .	133.33
Moore, W. A.......	25.00	Reeves, C. B.......	605.32
Morris, J. K........	150.00	Richards, R. V......	60.00
		Richards, J. W. A...	158.33
Naussau, M. D.......	666.64	Richards, Matilda A.	60.00
Nebo, A. S..........	272.00	Ricks, J. H.........	533.32
Nelson, D. C........	150.00	Roberts, James E. .	320.00
Nevins, G. N........	95.00	Roberts, J. W.......	24.14
Neufville, W........	145.00	Ross, A. N..........	75.00
North, Frances	37.50	Ross, Martha C.....	41.66
Norman, O. S.......	150.00	Ross, E. B..	125.00
		Ross, W. N........	465.96
Okai, R. F..........	28.80	Roland, T. N.......	150.00
Oost Afrika Co......	477.36	Russ, Alford.......	50.00
		Russell, F. A. K.....	1,072.00
Padmore, D. L.......	137.50	Russell, N. K......	22.00
Padmore, J. R. D....	258.30	Russell, M. N......	700.00
Page, Aaron A.	50.00		
Page, H. A..........	1,241.56	Scotland, John W...	24.00
Page, Lucy A.......	41.66	Scott, A. L........	40.00
Page, W. B..........	183.31	Scott, S. K........	272.00
Parker, James A.....	40.00	Sharpe, S. A........	100.00
Parker, Ida C........	400.00	Shaw, W. L........	34.00
Parker, P. C., Jr.....	166.66	Shannon, E. H......	700.00
Parson, P. C. F.....	22.50	Sherman, R. A......	605.32
Payne, Benjamin W..	225.00	Simpson, C. L......	724.98
Peabody, A. D.......	41.66	Simpson, Hettie....	40.00

Payments from unassigned revenues, January 1, 1932, to December 31, 1932 inclusive, listed alphabetically by names of payees.—Continued.

Name	Amount	Name	Amount
Simpson, Joseph.....	$22.50	Vampelt, M. T......	$133.34
Sims, J. E...........	45.00	Victor Radio Corp...	300.00
Smallwood, R. D.....	166.64		
Smith, James E......	81.00		
Smith, James S......	2,077.56	Walker, Arthur.....	120.00
Smith, Jos...........	108.00	Walker, E. D.......	22.50
Smith, M. C........	62.40	Walker, Isaac.......	140.00
Smythe, Hannah V...	170.83	Wallace, G. W......	262.50
Smythe, J. H.......	160.00	Ward, Thomas E....	168.75
Sottile, Antonio......	1,702.10	Ware, G. B........	41.66
So. American Cable.		Weaver, George....	100.00
Co...............	442.49	Wesley, Sarah H....	83.33
Spear, N. P.........	33.33	West & Co.........	292.46
Stevens, Gilbert.....	22.50	Wheaton, George...	40.00
Stryker, George......	25.00	Whitehead, Morris &	
Stryker, J. B........	605.32	Co...............	86.64
Stryker & Snetter....	63.20	White, H. M.......	20.83
Stubblefield, G. W....	375.26	White, H. L.......	605.32
Stubblefield, V. D....	375.00	White, J. R.........	605.32
Summerville, Edward.	166.66	Wiles, R. S........	533.32
		Williams, J. D......	20.83
Taylor, C. H........	288.70	Wilson, A. D., Jr....	272.00
Taylor, P. F........	99.80	Williams, T. E. K...	112.49
Taylor, S. J.........	300.00	Witherspoon, J. J...	623.32
Taylor, J. S. B......	41.66	Witherspoon, W. M.	623.32
Tisdell, J. B........	22.50	Woermann, A. & Co.	321.60
Thomas, J. T........	41.66	Woermann Line....	237.40
Thompson, S. A. D...	58.32	Worrell, D. A. B....	605.32
Tolbert, F. E........	100.00	Worrell, E. J. S.....	650.00
Tolbert, Mozart.....	25.00	Woods, E. Tyson...	145.81
Toliver, J. A........	20.83	Wright, Etta.......	233.32
Tappeh, George......	93.00		
Travell, W. A........	322.20		
Trinity, T. N........	40.00	Yancy, Allen N.....	95.83
Tubman, A. C.......	41.66		
Tunning, C. O.......	83.32	1,342 checks of $20.00	
Tucker, H. E........	183.32	and over—TOTAL.	$127,840.46
Twe, D.............	20.00	1,158 checks of less	
Tyler, W. H.........	601.30	than $20.00 each..	9,087.87
Tyler, Thomas H.....	22.50		
U. S. T. C. Bank		GRAND TOTAL OF ALL	
Charges, etc......	3,394.37	PAYMENTS.......	$136,928.33

Table completed on following page.

Correct Statement from the records of the Financial Adviser, R. L.

(signed)   W. A. TRAVELL,
Supervisor of Internal Revenue, R. L.

MONROVIA, LIBERIA,
February 3, 1933.

APPENDIX B

Sir John Simon to Sir R. Lindsay (Washington)
Foreign Office, May 29, 1934.

SIR,

His Majesty's Government in the United Kingdom have given earnest consideration to the situation which has arisen in Liberia owing to the refusal of the Liberian Government to accept the plan of assistance drawn up by the Special Committee appointed by the Council of the League of Nations. It is clear that, since the Liberian Government have maintained their obstructive attitude, no effective action is possible by the League of Nations to improve administration in Liberia and to ameliorate the treatment of the native tribes. As your Excellency is aware, His Majesty's Government have always desired to act in concert with the Government of the United States of America in the Liberian question, and they are anxious therefore to ascertain the views of the United States Government, and to explain their own, in the very unfortunate situation that has arisen.

2. Your Excellency will recall that it was in consequence of charges of slave trading in Liberia, made by certain American travellers that the present question first arose. In June 1929 the United States representative at Monrovia addressed a strong protest to the Liberian Government, which drew attention to the "development of a system hardly distinguishable from organised slave trade . . . in the enforcement of which the Liberian Frontier Force and the services and influence of certain high Government officials are constantly and systematically used." Mr. Francis's note also indicated that the Governments of the world might have to consider "some effective affirmative action . . . to terminate the situation" and drew attention to the "historic special interest of the United States in the welfare and progress of Liberia." The Liberian Government

208

repudiated the charges and asked the League to investigate the position. Accordingly, the Christie Commission was appointed, consisting of a United States citizen and a Liberian with a British chairman. The commission reported that the charges were fully borne out by the facts, and recommended in broad outline the reforms necessary to prevent the recurrence of the evils indicated. Thereupon the Liberian Government declared that their financial position was such that they could not carry out reforms of that character without the assistance of the League. The Council of the League then, with the approval and encouragement of the United States Government, appointed a committee to consider what financial assistance could be given to Liberia and upon what terms. At a very early stage of the enquiry it became clear that there was no hope of any financial assistance to Liberia unless the American Firestone interests, already engaged in a large scheme of Liberian development under which extensive control of Liberian finance had been at one time granted to them, was prepared to collaborate. The committee were further convinced that it would be improper and useless for the League to make itself in any degree responsible for assisting Liberia unless the administration of the country were put on a footing which afforded a guarantee of decent administration, especially of the native tribes. Accordingly the Brunot Commission was appointed to advise the committee in detail as to the administrative and financial changes in Liberia that were necessary in order to carry out the objects in view. Throughout it was insisted by the committee that no assistance to Liberia could be recommended unless she agreed to and carried out the reforms regarded as essential to secure decent administration. If she rejected these reforms she could have no assistance. What steps would then be necessary to enforce compliance with the obligation that rests on all members of the League to "secure just treatment of the native inhabitants of the territories under their control" was left over for later consideration. The committee, on which a representative of the United States Government sat, drew up a plan of assistance largely based on the recommendations of the Brunot Commission. Its main feature was the proposal to appoint a white Chief Adviser with certain assistants to supervise the essential administrative reforms. At the instance of the Firestone Company, supported by the representative of the United States Government the authority of the Chief Adviser was emphasised, it being rightly thought that, unless he was put in a position to insist on the execution of the reforms, there was little hope that anything effective would be done. On the basis of this plan the Firestone interest expressed their willingness to give considerable financial assistance to Liberia.

3. During the course of the enquiry in the autumn of 1931 trouble arose in the south of Liberia, in which certain of the Kru tribes were concerned. On the excuse of the alleged non-payment of taxes, what can only be described as a punitive expedition was despatched from Monrovia to the Kru coast. The reports which reached His Majesty's Government of the doings of this expedition were such that they not only addressed strong representations to the Liberian Government, but, with the concurrence of the United States, French and German Governments, despatched one of His Majesty's Consular Officers to the Kru coast in order to obtain an independent report. The effect of this report was to indicate that the Liberian forces had been guilty of grave excesses which resulted, not merely in the wanton destruction of villages, coupled with the driving of the tribal population into the bush, but in the slaughter of nearly 150 human beings—men, women and children. There had also been considerable fighting between the various tribes, which threatened to extend over the Grebo country still further to the south. At the instance of the Committee, a League Commissioner visited the district.

4. His visit, which was facilitated by the resources of His Majesty's Government, resulted, in the autumn of 1932, in the conclusion of a series of truces between the Liberian Government and the tribes on the one hand, and between the tribes themselves on the other, an arrangement which was accompanied by the collection of arms from the tribes and their deposit in Monrovia. These truces expired in the course of last year, and their expiry has been followed not only by the recurrence of inter-tribal feuds, which must be expected so long as fair and humane administration is withheld, but more recently by the despatch of another Government force from Monrovia, which, according to reports which His Majesty's Government feel compelled to credit, is conducting itself in a manner not

dissimilar from that adopted in 1932. Meanwhile, the arms of the tribes have not been returned to them. The especial urgency of the situation lies in these facts.

5. To sum up. Greatly to the regret of His Majesty's Government, the League's attempt to assist Liberia has not been successful. Liberia rejected, on the financial side, the not ungenerous terms obtained for her by the League from her chief foreign creditor, the Finance Corporation of America. Indeed, she has, I understand, repudiated most of her obligations to that body. On the administrative side she made reservations which, if accepted, would render it impossible for the white officials, who were to be appointed under the League plan, to secure any serious administrative reform. In these circumstances the League Council have felt impelled to withdraw the plan of assistance offered to Liberia, and His Majesty's Government feel that the whole situation must be reconsidered. They feel that it would be a dereliction of duty to civilisation if the misgovernment of the native tribes by Liberia were to be allowed to continue, resulting, as it would infallibly result, in the encouragement of such evils as slave trading and the slaughter and maltreatment of the 2 million natives by the corrupt and inefficient oligarchy of Monrovia. At the same time His Majesty's Government cannot believe that the pressure of public opinion, or even the threat of exclusion of Liberia from the League, if that should be practicable, will be adequate to create any real and lasting improvement in Liberia. They are aware of the deep interest which the United States Government have always taken in the fortunes of this State, which, indeed, owes its foundation to American enterprise and philanthropy. On the material side, Liberia is rendered dependent upon the United States Government by the extent to which her financial machinery is already in American hands and organised in conformity with a contract entered into between the Liberian Government and an American Corporation. His Majesty's Government cannot, therefore, doubt that the United States Government have been as much perturbed as have they themselves by the course of recent events, and they would be grateful for an indication of the policy which the United States Government would in the circumstances recommend. For their own part, His Majesty's Government are ready to co-operate to

the utmost of their power in any well-considered measures which the United States Government may consider appropriate to the occasion.

6. The enclosed copy of the minutes of the recently concluded session of the League Council (20) will serve to complete for Your Excellency the picture of the present situation, of which the United States Government, who were again represented at Geneva by Mr. Reber, will no doubt be fully informed. I shall be glad if you will address to the United States Government a note on the lines of the preceding paragraphs.

I am, &c.

JOHN SIMON.